The Massey Lectures Series

The Massey Lectures are co-sponsored by CBC Radio, House of Anansi Press, and Massey College in the University of Toronto. The series was created in honour of the Right Honourable Vincent Massey, former governor general of Canada, and was inaugurated in 1961 to provide a forum on radio where major contemporary thinkers could address important issues of our time.

This book comprises the 2006 Massey Lectures, "The Ethical Imagination," broadcast in November 2006 as part of CBC Radio's *Ideas* series. The producer of the series was Philip Coulter; the executive producer was Bernie Lucht.

Margaret Somerville

Margaret Somerville is Samuel Gale Professor of Law, Professor in the Faculty of Medicine, and Founding Director of the Centre for Medicine, Ethics and Law at McGill University, Montreal. She has an extensive national and international publishing and speaking record and is a frequent commentator in all forms of media. She is deeply committed to the public's right to be involved in the decision-making shaping our society. To this end, she wrote *The Ethical Canary: Science, Society and the Human Spirit* and *Death Talk: the Case against Euthanasia and Physician-Assisted Suicide.* She has edited *Do We Care? Renewing Canada's Commitment to Health* (Proceedings of the first Directions for Canadian Health Care conference); and co-edited *Transdisciplinarity: reCreating Integrated Knowledge.* Professor Somerville is a regular consultant, nationally and internationally, to a wide variety of bodies including governments, United Nations organizations, and NGOs, especially regarding ethics and public policy, and has served on many editorial boards, advisory boards, and boards of directors. She has received many honours and awards, including the Order of Australia, and honorary doctorates in law and in science. In 2003 she became the first recipient of the UNESCO Avicenna Prize for Ethics in Science.

The
Ethical
Imagination

Journeys of the Human Spirit

Margaret Somerville

ANANSI

Published in 2006 by
House of Anansi Press Inc.
110 Spadina Avenue, Suite 801
Toronto, ON, M5V 2K4
Tel. 416-363-4343
Fax 416-363-1017
www.anansi.ca

Distributed in Canada by
HarperCollins Canada Ltd.
1995 Markham Road
Scarborough, ON, M1B 5M8
Toll free tel. 1-800-387-0117

CBC and Massey College logos used with permission

10 09 08 07 06   1 2 3 4 5

LIBRARY AND ARCHIVES CANADA CATALOGUING IN PUBLICATION DATA

Somerville, Margaret A., 1942–
The ethical imagination / Margaret Somerville.

(CBC Massey lectures)
Includes bibliographical references and index.
ISBN-13: 978-0-88784-747-9
ISBN-10: 0-88784-747-1

I. Title. II. Series.

BJ1581.2.S65 2006   170'.44   C2006-903674-8

Cover design: Bill Douglas
Typesetting: Brian Panhuyzen

Canada Council   Conseil des Arts
for the Arts   du Canada

ONTARIO ARTS COUNCIL
CONSEIL DES ARTS DE L'ONTARIO

We acknowledge for their financial support of our publishing program the Canada Council for the Arts, the Ontario Arts Council, and the Government of Canada through the Book Publishing Industry Development Program (BPIDP).

Printed and bound in Canada

For my dear aunt, Veronica Mary Rowe,

*who continues to teach me how to embrace life
no matter what it brings,*

with love and gratitude.

Let us give birth to the unexpected
So hope for a great sea-change
On the far side of revenge
Believe that a farther shore
Is reachable from here.
Believe in miracles and cures and healing wells.

— from *Cure of Troy*, Seamus Heaney

Contents

I

GOING ON THE ETHICAL WALLABY:

SEARCHING FOR A SHARED ETHICS

COMMON HUMANITY AND universal responsibility link us. But much of the time we act as if this is not the case — we are in denial as individuals and societies. In the past, our denial harmed those whose plight we ignored. Today it harms everyone, which is why we, the deniers, can no longer afford it — if, indeed, we ever could.

I believe that one way to promote the change we need is to find a shared ethics. Such a search will help us to start from and emphasize what we have in common. When we simply took that commonality for granted, we could afford the luxury of starting from and focusing on our disagreements, but this is no longer our situation. Searching for a shared ethics will also help us to identify those, such as terrorists and tyrants, with whom we have serious, fundamental value conflicts that threaten individuals and societies. It will be far from a complete solution to the world's problems — nothing can be. But I believe it will help.

This book is about searching for a shared ethics for an interdependent world — that is, as British Prime Minister Tony Blair suggests[1], a world in which a crisis somewhere is necessarily a crisis elsewhere and, sometimes, everywhere. In other words, it is about trying to find those values we hold in common and imagining how we might go about doing so. And it is about the importance of stories, myths, poetry, imagination, "examined emotions," intuition — especially moral intuition — and the human spirit to human ethics. It's not that reason, common sense, objective facts, and science are unimportant to ethics — on the contrary. Rather, the problem is that they are often assumed to be the *only* matters important to ethics. Because I adamantly disagree, I've decided to take you on a journey, one that I hope might convince you of the importance of using the full richness of our human ways of knowing to "do ethics" in our contemporary societies.

In *The Ethical Canary*[2], a book I wrote a few years ago, I proposed two foundational principles for a shared ethics: deep respect for all life, in particular human life; and profound respect for the human spirit. In this present book, I'm putting forward two concepts that I believe can help us to implement those principles: recognizing and developing a sense of the sacred that we can all share — the *secular sacred*; and adopting a basic presumption in favour of the natural as the starting point for our decision-making about ethics. I believe that together these principles and concepts can help us to realize two closely linked goals: finding a shared ethics, and generating the hope — the oxygen of the human spirit — that is essential for our humanity.

At the deepest level, there's nothing really new about what I'm arguing. Mine is an argument about the sacred in the sense that something that is sacred deserves deep respect; that the natural and nature are among those matters we regard as sacred; that we must search for the ethical behavior we need to implement the required respect; and that we must wisely express these requirements in the matrix of law that we construct to define and defend our humanity. All of these are human aspirations that go back at least as far as we have records.

If you were a lawyer, you would think from what I've just written that I belong to what is called the Natural Law school of jurisprudence. To some extent that is correct, although there is an important difference between my thinking and that of classic Natural Law adherents. As you will read throughout this book, like them, I believe there are some innate fundamental principles that can guide us, and we must find them. But unlike them, I believe that we can find and agree on some of those principles whether or not we have a belief in the supernatural or are religious.[3] Where I part company with those who disagree with me over the ethics and law that should govern issues addressed in this book such as human embryo research, genetic manipulation, or same-sex marriage, is that I believe these matters have at their core a natural reality and that the ethics and law we use to govern them must respect that reality. In other words, ethics and law are not just social constructs; I believe that they need to be expressive of the deepest truths of human nature.

Throughout the years as I have worked on the most avant-garde issues at the frontiers of medicine and science, time and time again I've found that I needed to go far back in human history to try to come to an understanding of how we might face the future ethically and legally. In this book I am suggesting that we need to revisit a very old concept of ethics and an earlier idea of law, to find what we need to construct a shared ethics that can guide us.

Currently, some of the most challenging and unprecedented ethical issues are raised by the new technoscience: genetics, reproductive technologies, artificial intelligence, robotics, nanotechnology, and so on. A major focus of this book is on those issues. My goal, however, is not just to explore the immediate and direct ethical issues related to researching, developing, and using the new technoscience, important as these are, but also to show that this technoscience raises ethical controversies that go to the very roots of what it means to be human, how we relate to others and our world, and how we find meaning in life.

I agonized about which topics to include, and the choices I made are not neutral with respect to either the factors that influenced them or their impact. I have long argued that "doing ethics" is an exercise of power because people act or refrain from acting on the basis of the arguments and reasoning ethicists put forward. Therefore, "doing ethics" carries the responsibility, as does every exercise of power, to act ethically. The ethics of "doing ethics" in any given situation must also be assessed to safeguard the process of "doing ethics" from abuse. There is almost no literature on the ethics of ethicists — they are simply presumed to be ethical. But we cannot afford to take that for granted and, like everyone who exercises power or influence over others — priests, politicians, police officers, professors, publishers, company executives, lawyers, judges, journalists, or scientists — they too *must* act ethically. In short, the ethicist confronts ethics on two levels: in the ethical challenges that arise out of a given situation, and in the ethical responsibility that comes with the exercise of power.

The ethics of doing ethics includes assessing the ethics of our choices to highlight some issues as important and, likewise, leave others in the shadows. We know from research that ideas about which ethical issues and values are most important differ by socio-economic class. The affluent see the ethics that should govern science and technology as the most important issue; the poor believe that the ethics of dealing with drug addiction, abortion, and discrimination should be given priority.[4] And even those choices reflect the differing priorities only of people in Western societies.

Some of the most important ethical issues in our world concern justice and equity between people in developing countries and developed ones —such as access to food and clean water, shelter, physical safety, and basic health care. These problems are experienced as truly overwhelming, not only by people in developing countries who face them in their daily lives, but also by people in developed countries who as a result feel paralyzed to help, which is itself a problem. I want to make it absolutely clear that in not addressing those issues in this book, in no way do I want to detract from their immense importance and the ethical necessity for all of us to address them.

At first glance you might also think that the new technoscience is not the place to start looking for a shared ethics such as I propose we need. I believe my choice can be justified on five grounds. First, science has no territorial boundaries, and, consequently, the ethical issues it raises in one country are likely to be faced in many others. Second, what is done with science in one country can have a major impact on others. In other words, the ethics of the new science is both directly and indirectly relevant to developing countries. Third, developing countries might have to make difficult ethical decisions about whether to use the new science (and to take on any risks or harms that doing so, or not doing so, entails) in order to address the ethical problems they face in relation to access to food and clean water, shelter, physical safety, and basic health care. Fourth, the new science raises divisive issues going to the heart of some of our most important human values. In doing so, it forces us to look for common ground in ways that few other matters do. And fifth, if we can find a shared ethics to govern the new science, we might use it as a model for finding a shared ethics in a much broader sphere of activities.

Later on, I want to take up the topic of a *shared ethics*, but I want to explain briefly here what I mean by that term and the sense in which I will use it in this book. I am speaking of establishing a base or starting point that consists of ethical concepts and values that we already share and on which we can build; I am not suggesting that we all have to agree on everything. Rather, I'm looking for limited areas where some of us can agree. What those areas are will vary from group to group. The idea is to find what we have in common ethically so that we can experience ourselves as belonging to the same moral community. Engaging in a collective search to find those limited areas is likely to produce greater agreement. It is also realistic: getting all of us to agree on everything is a utopian goal, but it's not a realistic one in our fragmented world. I believe it is important to have realizable goals in ethics and to avoid the disappointments that unrealizable ones create. Such disappointments are not neutral in their impact; they are harmful because they result in loss of hope, and cynicism.

The Challenge of Science to the Human Spirit

Today's mind-altering, world-altering scientific breakthroughs are challenging our ancient human philosophical-spiritual heritage in unprecedented ways. I use the term *human philosophical-spiritual heritage* in the largest possible sense — as encompassing all of our most important shared values, attitudes, principles, and beliefs, whatever their source. And further, I regard spirituality as a natural, inherent characteristic common to all humans, which some express through religious belief and practice, and others express in secular ways. We can call our capacity to experience that spirituality the "human spirit." It is the intangible, immeasurable, numinous reality that all of us need to find meaning in life and to make life worth living — a deeply intuitive sense of relatedness or connectedness to all life, especially other people, to the world, and to the universe in which we live. One manifestation of the human spirit or human spirituality is the longing for transcendence — the strong desire to experience the feeling of belonging to something larger than ourselves.

Some people see the new technoscience — for instance, genetics — as challenging the existence of the human spirit. That depends on how we view that science. I believe that it is likely we will find that our capacity to experience what I am calling the human spirit has a genetic base that probably must be initially turned on by particular kinds of experience. But in saying this, I am not supporting genetic determinism or genetic reductionism — that is, that we and all our experiences are nothing more than the functioning of our genes. Rather, I believe our genetic makeup might be a necessary substratum that opens up the possibility of having a wide variety of experiences of the human spirit that, otherwise, might not be available to us.

One response to resolving the challenges unprecedented scientific breakthroughs present to our human spirit is to abandon the science (religious fundamentalists take this route) or to abandon the philosophical-spiritual heritage (pure rationalists' chosen path). In other words, the people at each pole adopt the same strategy to reconcile what they perceive as a conflict between science and our philosophical-spiritual heritage, although the content of what they abandon is the opposite. I believe it is a tragic mistake to abandon either body of knowledge. Rather, we need a new vision that can facilitate the marriage of science and our human philosophical-spiritual heritage, and support the continuance of that marriage. One way to find that vision is by searching for a shared ethics. But we cannot set out on our search for a shared ethics without a vision. We need two visions that are related, in that each generates the other, but are not the same — the ancient symbol of the snake swallowing its tail tells us of such symbiotic situations. And that means that we need imagination, because it is a fundamental way in which we can have access to vision.

Let's now look at the building blocks for a shared ethics: imagination; stories; the role of ethicists and the nature of doing ethics; our ways of knowing; human ethics; articulating the concept of a shared ethics; basic presumptions; and the source and nature of ethics.

The First Building Block: Imagination

Imagination is the door to amazement, which British-American theologian Alan Jones describes as the primordial way of looking at the world. Religion (or for some people, spirituality), science, and ethics are all journeys of the human imagination; and the spiritual or mystical imagination, the scientific imagination, and the moral imagination are all linked. As moral theologian Ronald Rolheiser says, the purpose of the mystical imagination (and I would add, the moral imagination) "is to help us see, understand, imagine, speak about, and relate to reality — in particular, reality or realities that cannot be perceived directly through our senses — in a way beyond fantasy and superstition." Both these imaginations show us things "that science, wonderful though it is, cannot."[5] The mystical imagination can show us the many realities — for instance, love — that are not perceived directly by our physical senses. The moral imagination allows us access to concepts of good and evil, and right and wrong — that is, access to the domain of another intangible, the human conscience. Ethics in science involves a combination of the mystical, moral, and scientific imaginations. I use the term *the ethical imagination* to encompass all three.

But not everyone values the mystical imagination. Nobel Prize winner and co-discoverer of DNA James Watson once said to me, "The problem with you, Margo, is that you're full of mystical nonsense." I related this incident to Ronald Rolheiser, who said: "Yes, there is always the danger of 'mystical nonsense,' but there is, I believe, an even greater danger in being 'mystically tone-deaf.' The older I get, the more I become sure of only one thing: we understand a lot less than we think, and the mystics like John of the Cross got it right when they said, 'Learn to understand more by not understanding than by understanding!'"[6]

I often think about *what* we don't know *that* we don't know in terms of a colony of ants. I've watched fascinated as these insects go about their work and lives, often building complex structures that rival the Egyptian pyramids in architecture and geographic orientation. That colony is their universe. And yet we humans know that there is another universe beyond theirs, the universe that we comprehend. It seems to me disingenuous to flatly deny that there could be a universe beyond the one we know, another universe that comprehends us as we do the little universe of ants, a universe that we, in our turn, can't hope to comprehend. Being human, however, unlike the ants, perhaps we might at least admit the possibility of worlds beyond our knowledge.

All journeys of our imaginations involve both our individual imaginations and our shared (or collective) human imagination. And in religion, science, and ethics, others must believe and accept the "results" that emerge from those journeys in order to establish the integrity and authenticity of these results. In short, imagination is a shared means of access to religion or spirituality, science, and ethics and, therefore, is a link between them. Moreover, throughout our history the mystical and scientific imaginations have been intimately linked, but lately we seem to have lost our awareness of that. Indeed, some modern scientists adamantly deny that such a link — or the mystical imagination itself — exists. But might the mystical imagination and its link to the scientific imagination have been what Albert Einstein was getting at when he said, "We all dance to a mysterious tune, intoned in the distance by an invisible player"? I believe that seeking a shared ethics might be one way to write the score for some cadences of that "mysterious tune." And scientists may be among our best composers. What astrophysics, for example, is telling us about the music of the heavens gives us access to tunes no humans before us have ever heard.

A traditional southern and western African greeting is, "What do you dance?" This question can teach us about searching for a shared ethics. It assumes that we all dance. It asks, "*What* do you dance?" not "*Do* you dance?"; it includes everyone. Likewise, we should ask, "What ethics do you dance?" not "Do you have ethics?" The question also assumes that dancing is innate to humans, as I believe morality is, but that we do not all dance the same dance. Likewise, it assumes that we hear music to dance to, but we do not all hear the same music. And, very importantly, it assumes that we can describe to one another what music we hear and what dance we do, and, as a result, identify where we are the same and where we differ. And if others want to learn our dance or we theirs, that knowledge can be transmitted.

In the past, a given group or society found and undertook the journey of the collective human imagination through religion. That is, among other functions, a shared religion carried the community's collective imagination. This situation has changed in two ways: First, in our modern interconnected world, the collectivity involved in searching for a shared ethics is everyone, not just one isolated community. When our local community comprised "the world," a shared religion bound that community together. Now the entire world — literally — is our local community. We do not have a universally shared religion in that community. Indeed, in addition to our myriad of religious traditions, some of us are not religious. If we cannot use religion, then how do we find our collective imagination and bind ourselves together? Can a purely secular approach replace religion in this matter? For instance, many people focus on science as a substitute for religion — or even as a "secular religion"[7] — it too promises "miracles" and life extension. But can science alone truly carry the collective imagination?

I want to emphasize that in asking whether a secular approach can replace some traditional functions of religion, I am not buying into the secularist argument that religion has no place in the public square, or at least nothing valuable to contribute, or certainly nothing valuable beyond the purely private sphere. I do not agree, but I recognize that religion cannot function in the public square in the same way as it did in the past. I believe we must be careful not to blindly accept the secularists' proclamations of the "death of religion." We often speak of "secular" Western societies, in contrast to religious ones in other parts of the world. But, at the risk of overgeneralization, while it is true that Europe is overwhelmingly secular — only a small minority of people attends church with any consistency — a large majority of Americans identify themselves as religious, many attend Church regularly and consider religion to be an important part of their lives. Canada falls somewhere in between. Consequently, religion, just like secularism and atheism, must be accommodated as part of the process of finding a shared ethics. Moreover, many people who say they are not religious simultaneously claim to be spiritual. In short, by the term *secular society* I mean one in which law and public policy are not based directly on religion. I specifically do not mean a society in which religious and spiritual voices are excluded from the public sphere.

As I was musing about the connections among imagination, vision, and a shared ethics, I came across a short statement written by Philip Carter, an Anglican priest who is the director of the Julian Centre (an ecumenical Christian centre for spirituality) in Adelaide, Australia. Speaking of the search for peace, Carter says:

> Perhaps the greatest impediment to peace is a failure of nerve, a lack of imagination. What if we could hear the echo in the human heart of a vision which haunts and lures us — a vision which is the true source of life and its goal — a vision of a deeper communion. . . . The Australian poet, Kevin Hart, has written a little Haiku poem:
>
> *Each day forces us*
> *to totter on planks we hope*
> *will become bridges.*
>
> Those planks don't seem much; for some they won't be enough. Of course this little poem lacks the rhetoric of the quick fix, the easy answer. But the "planks we hope will become bridges" are real, and small, and within our grasp, and this image exposes an inner stubbornness, a resolute willingness to work with what is and at the same time to be captured by something more. Our future is beckoning, and it shapes us even more than our past.
>
> Is it possible to let go of the self-defeating parables we too often tell ourselves, and to live out of and into the vision of a deeper communion?

I cannot be me without you
and we cannot be us without them,
and together we have a future.[8]

Of course, Carter's words can be read as religious, and they almost certainly are. But they are also highly relevant to those who reject religion as an informing principle in their lives or societies. Carter links imagination, vision, bonding, acceptance of uncertainty, courage, fortitude, and hope — "the beckoning future" — all of which are essential attributes of those who would search for a shared human ethics for our world.

Humans share their imaginations and bond with one another through the stories they tell. A story is to human growth as a fact is to science, mathematics is to physics, or poetry is to the human spirit. Myths are a special kind of story. They capture and express realities that cannot be put directly into words and shared in any other way. Mythologist Joseph Campbell maintained that what is common to all humanity is the experience of awe and wonder (experiences that he would call religious) and the resulting creation of myths that help give our lives meaning and purpose. That is experiencing awe and wonder, and creating myths are cause and effect. Myths allow us to communicate about intangible realities that cannot be communicated in any other way. Myths are not literally true, but they do not represent untruths, lies, or fantasies; they are metaphorically true and often are the only way to communicate the truth they represent. Myths have a role to play in ethics, not least because they are the product of imagination. They have long been important tools in the search to answer questions such as What does it mean to be human?, What am I doing here?, What is the meaning of life?, Where do I fit in the cosmos? They are also the storehouse of some of our most ancient knowledge. The word *myth* is also used in two other senses: First, to describe something that is not a factual reality but, rather, a fantasy — for instance, the myth of the "1950s nuclear family." Despite being, at least to some extent, fantasies, such myths still matter and play an important role in our individual and collective lives. Second, the word *myth* can also be used as a synonym for a falsehood or lie.

One danger to avoid in ethics is the confusion of myths that carry deep truths with those that are either fantasies or lies. We encounter a similar danger when we use the word *imagination*, or describe how we see imagination and that to which it gives us access. That which we find through imagination is not imaginary in the sense that it is non-existent. Rather, imagination is a way of knowing that we can use to gain access to, and explore, numinous realities. The experience of these realities is not available to us through reason or logic and cannot be verified by the latter means, because such realities are of a different order or kind. What we learn through them is not inconsistent with reason and logic, just different. To give an example, we might all agree that science can tell us that evolution occurred, but we disagree about whether evolution can be attributed to an Intelligent Designer — that is, whether it occurred by chance or choice. The latter is a question of a different kind from the former, one which cannot be answered by science and, therefore, should not be taught *as science* in the classroom. A discussion of the theory of intelligent design is relevant, however, to the philosophy of science. Put another way, science can establish the fact that evolution occurred, but not why. For some of us, the latter question can be answered by using imagination as a gateway to a different kind of human experience and knowledge. Some people call that knowledge Faith.

The Second Building Block: Stories

So far in these pages I have emphasized that we need to search for what we have in common in order to find a base for a shared ethics. But, in fact, in ethics, identifying our differences is just as important. Both what we share *and* what separates us can lead to ethical insights that would otherwise be unavailable. Stories allow us to buy into and share our communal imaginative experience, whether that experience is generated by exploring the wilderness together, sitting around a campfire, going to the opera, ballet, a rock concert, watching the Olympics or hockey, or attending church, temple, or synagogue.

I'd like to share with you a story about the search for a title for this book. When I began writing, I considered calling these lectures "On the Ethical Wallaby." That title appealed to me for several reasons. My family on both sides comes from the Outback of Australia. As a child I often heard my parents or uncles or aunts say, "Oh, he's gone 'on the wallaby'!" In Aussie vernacular, that saying meant a man (it was always a man) had set off into the Bush and was walking from farm to farm or station to station, looking for work. This practice had started in the Great Depression and may well have roots in the Australian Aboriginal tradition of "going Walkabout." The men "on the wallaby" were following the trails the wallabies make as they move from waterhole to waterhole in the semi-arid areas that border the Great Australian Desert. The men knew they would find farms and stations in following these trails because the wallabies were always travelling toward water, and it was only at homesteads that water was brought up from the deep artesian basin for livestock to drink. These men "on the wallaby" were independent, tough, resilient, and self-reliant. The money they earned was often sent home to support their families.

So the image came to my mind of being "on the ethical wallaby." My career in ethics has been a journey along many tracks, some well marked, others barely visible; some leading to expected places, others into unknown territory; some leading to intellectually rich opportunities for "ethics work," others toward scarce resources and barriers to ethics; some going forward to a ready welcome, others to an instantly slammed door. And just as men went "on the wallaby" to try to deal with a scarcity of economic resources, perhaps we are doing the ethical equivalent of that today because of a scarcity of shared moral resources.

The title resonated for me in another way too. Some years ago I was driving through the Australian bush in a car without air conditioning on a very hot (plus 40°c) day. My yellow Labrador dog, Henri, was leaning out the open back window to catch the breeze when suddenly he hurled himself through it, rolled on the road, picked himself up, put his nose to the ground, and zigzagged off into the eucalyptus scrub. Not far ahead, I could see a mob of kangaroos making a fast exit. Like all Labradors, Henri was primarily using his nose, not his eyes. He was moving in an erratic way, following the scent of the zigzag path that the kangaroos had taken — they, like wallabies, often bound from side to side. It was a much longer route for my dog than a direct one would have been, but accurate none the less. Often, I think, we need to do the same in ethics; we cannot go directly to the target. Indeed, trying to do so can limit our ethical knowledge. Moreover, in order to find what we need, depending upon the situation we are dealing with, we may need to give priority to one of our senses or ways of knowing over another — much like my dog did.

This same idea about our need to accept indirectness and its companions — engaging in watchful waiting, and living comfortably with uncertainty in order to gain insight, especially ethical insight — is captured in a much more dramatic and poetic fashion by the novelist E. M. Forster when he "distinguishes 'the development of the novel,' which is the same as the 'development of humanity,' from the 'great tedious onrush known as history.' The latter [he says] includes 'trifles' which 'belong to history not to art'; Forster's examples of such trifles are the taming of the atom, landing on the moon, and abolishing warfare. The former is 'a shy crablike sideways movement' towards tenderness, the tenderness which connection makes possible."⁹ I suggest that there is a connection between indirectness and its companions, on the one hand, and, on the other, tenderness. Both require that in seeking to reach our goals, we exercise restraint and accept uncertainty rather than seeking our goals through force and domination — in short, we must make ourselves vulnerable, including to failure.

Those Australian men "on the wallaby" were following a trail laid out by nature. I believe we need to do the same in searching for a shared ethics, and I believe we can do so by recognizing the importance of a basic presumption in favour of the natural. We should not restrict ourselves to that trail, but we must identify it, and know when we are on it and when we are not, and where we ought to be.

The humans "on the wallaby" — like the wallabies themselves — were in search of the necessities of life, that which they needed to survive. I believe the same is true of our search for a shared ethics. Whether we can find what we seek is likely to be a determining factor in our survival and that of our planet. Finding a shared ethical base in a pluralistic, multicultural, global society is not optional; it is crucial to our survival physically and morally. The challenge is to find consensus in diversity and difference, and to retain the breadth, depth, and richness of human knowing, including that kind of knowing most of us traditionally found, but now only some of us find, through religion.

This book contains the stories of some of the people, places of the mind and spirit, intellectual and emotional adventures, ideas and learning I've encountered on the trail. My hope is that it will be useful as a catalyst; I believe it will be important only to the extent that it can act as a template to allow others to interact and create new ethical knowledge, and perhaps wisdom.

A Chinese proverb ("A bird does not sing because it has an answer. It sings because it has a song") captures how I hope this book might function. In the same vein, I hope the cover of this book, as well as the words and ideas within, might stimulate insights. For me, the bird on the man's shoulder symbolizes the human spirit, imagination, freedom, and the capacity and courage to explore physical, intellectual, and spiritual unknowns. The bird looks quite old and scruffy — she has travelled far and faced many trials and challenges. She appears alert, questioning, and wise. Traditionally, wisdom comes with age and many journeys of the human spirit. It's hard to tell whether the bird is a pigeon (a messenger bird) or a dove (the symbol of harmony, love, and peace), but in either case, she's an ordinary, everyday bird. As such, she carries the message that all of us, not just a "chosen few," need to exercise our ethical imaginations and engage in journeys of the human spirit. In the ancient mythology of some societies — for instance, the tribes of the Sepik River Valley in New Guinea — a giant bird attached to the back of the head of either a woman or an androgynous figure symbolized the origins of life. The bird — a slang word for a woman in the Australian vernacular — reminds the postmodern man, who here represents humankind, that with the new technoscience we now hold the essence of life in the palm of our collective human hand and, with this, the future of our planet.

The Third Building Block: The Role of Ethicists and the Nature of "Doing Ethics"

As an ethicist, I find it is quite common to encounter people who are hostile to ethicists in general and, sometimes, to oneself in particular. These people (not uncommonly scientists) perceive ethicists as "moral police" telling them what and what not to do, and seriously curtailing what they see as their rights and freedoms. They believe ethicists impose their own moral values, more or less in the guise of secular priests, and they rightly challenge why ethicists' values should prevail when those values are no more important than others' values, and especially when there is no consensus on which values should prevail.

People who are critical of ethicists are correct in their criticism if ethicists are simply imposing their own personal, moral, and ethical values. It is not their right to do that and not the role of an ethicist to make decisions that others should make. Rather, it is the role of an ethicist to help those people who must make decisions about ethics to understand as fully as possible the nature of these decisions.

This requires that ethicists, first, help people to recognize that they might have an ethical problem — many ethical mistakes are made because people do not identify that there is a problem, or if they do recognize there is a problem, they mistakenly identify it as a public relations or communications issue and call in experts in these fields. That often substantially augments the seriousness and number of ethical issues involved. "Spin doctoring" an ethical issue is usually disastrous ethically. Often it means that what began as one ethical problem ends up as a host of problems.[10]

Second, once an ethical problem is identified, it is an ethicist's job to help the people who must make a decision analyze it in such a way that they can access the necessary ethical insights. That requires, first, knowing as many facts as possible about the situation, including any uncertainties — that "good facts are essential to good ethics" is a truism in ethics, but no less important because of that. Then the ethicist must help people to identify the ethical issues those facts raise and the different values that could inform their decisions. I sometimes describe the process by using the metaphor of a folded fan that must be unfolded. The ethicist helps the decision-maker to open the fan, identify the struts — the different lines of ethical analysis — whether the fan has multiple scenes or one picture painted on it, and the values relevant to that picture or those scenes. The next step is to see whether any of the relevant values conflict — if they don't, there is no ethical problem. All values can be honoured.

If the values conflict, however, they must be prioritized. Ethicists do not agree on how we should go about doing that and, depending on which approach is used, what we regard as ethical or unethical be radically different. There are two main camps of ethicists: Utilitarians assess ethical acceptability by seeing if potential goods outweigh risks and harms; a common way they assess that is by searching for the greatest good for the greatest number of people. One contemporary strand of utilitarianism can be described as moral relativism, insofar as the adherents of this approach deny the absoluteness or inherent rightness or wrongness of any given principle, and argue instead that all principles are culturally constructed. In doing so, they deny the existence of any moral order beyond that which humans create; in particular, they avoid the need to refer to any superhuman or supernatural entity as a source of ethics and morality. In stark contrast, principle-based or deontological ethicists believe that some things are wrong no matter how much good could come from them, and therefore these things must not be done. Their first consideration is whether any given course of conduct is, in itself, inherently wrong. Many principle-based ethicists found such judgements on concepts of a Natural Law or Natural Morality, which may or may not be seen as emanating from a supernatural or divine source.

When thinking about the ethical acceptability of any specific use of science and technology, utilitarians will ask, "What are the risks and benefits?" Some people criticize this as reducing ethics to nothing more than risk assessment. Principle-based ethicists will first ask what must we, may we, or must we not do with this science and technology in light of human integrity and human ends, and, likewise, the integrity of nature and the ends of nature. If this analysis shows it is not inherently wrong to use the science and technology, only then do these ethicists weigh risks and benefits.

In short, moral relativists argue there are no actions that can be described as "inherently" wrong; principle-based ethicists believe there are. To describe something as inherently wrong is, of course, a value judgement. But in my view this does not mean there is no substantive reality to a principle of inherent wrongness, or no substantive base on which to found it. For instance, most people agree that torture and slavery are inherently wrong no matter how much good might result from employing them. In other words, if something is inherently wrong it must not be undertaken, no matter how much good could result. Desmond Manderson, a McGill professor of law, language, and contemporary philosophy, puts it this way: "Ethics means that there are some things you do not do *even though* it would advantage you (or the whole society) to do them." He is saying here what principle-based ethicists believe: sometimes "being good" must take priority over "doing good." Put another way: it's not enough for an outcome to be ethically acceptable or even desirable; the means used to achieve it must also be ethical.

The example of torture indicates that there are ways other than reliance on a supernatural or divine source to find a substantive reality on which to base inherent wrongness. If, no matter which approach to ethics we work from, there is universal or nearly universal agreement that something is inherently wrong, we can regard that consensus as providing a substantive base for the authenticity of our judgement that it is wrong. Alternatively, the source of our agreement that something is inherently wrong is seen by some philosophers as an innate feature of human nature — that is, we are by nature a "moral animal."

Another way to look at the differences between the different camps of ethicists is articulated by the British philosopher Roger Scruton:

> "[T]he moral life rests . . . on three pillars: value, virtue and duty. Some hold that all the weight can be made to rest on only one of them: value, according to utilitarians; duty, according to their deontological opponents. . . . [But] we cannot give a coherent account of the moral life without doing justice to all the conceptions that support it — to value, virtue and duty — and showing their place, for human beings, in the good life."[11]

Scruton says that what is left out of contemporary standard treatments of ethics is the requirement to "face the surrounding world with due reverence and humility"[12] — a disposition he calls piety. I agree with him on all counts — although what he calls piety I'd call respecting the secular sacred, a concept I explore later. If we accept Scruton's tripartite base, perhaps many of the differences between us in matters of ethics occur because of differences in the order of priority that we give to value, virtue, and duty. Differences in the order are important because they can dramatically affect the decisions we make about ethics, but they comprise less of a difference than if we have no shared elements at all in our base. In my experience, believing that the latter is true — that we have no shared elements — is not uncommon in "doing ethics."

Whatever base we use for finding a shared ethics, one constant challenge is to identify conduct that we can all agree is ethically wrong. If none of the alternatives relevant to a particular situation are inherently wrong, then the principle-based ethicists and utilitarians can proceed together to assess the risks, harms, benefits, and potential benefits of each of the options that are or should be available. The decision-maker must then prioritize these options. If that prioritization results in some values being breached, the last step in the process is to find ethical justification for breaching the values that are not honoured. This is at the heart of doing ethics — its essence. It's the job of the ethicist to help people to work through this process, to make their decision, and to articulate their justification for that choice. It is precisely *not* the ethicist's job to make that decision in their stead.

It is also the role of ethicists to make available to people concepts that can reduce harms such as bitterness, hostility, and further exacerbations of destructive conflict. Take, for instance, the concept of "moral regret" — the idea that if we justifiably contravene someone's moral, ethical, or religious beliefs, in some circumstances we should express moral regrets for doing so. That is very different from simply contravening those beliefs and stating that one is right and justified in doing so. At times, there is no place for moral regrets about a stance one has taken. At other times, ethically we should regret contravening people's beliefs, even when we might disagree with those beliefs. We should always have respect for persons, if not their beliefs.

The Fourth Building Block: Ways of Knowing

Over the years I've found that sometimes people have the impression that I think that imagination is the master key to doing ethics. So I want to be clear about what I believe about what we can call "human ways of knowing." I believe such ways of knowing are multiple and diverse, and encompass the mind, body, heart, and spirit. John Ralston Saul in his Massey Lectures[13] introduced us to some of our ways of knowing — common sense; human memory (history); imagination and creativity; intuition (I'd emphasize moral intuition); reason and ethics — and explored some of them more fully in *On Equilibrium*.[14] I would emphasize experiential knowledge and underline its importance to ethics, because it cuts across all of the other ways of knowing used in "doing ethics." As well, we can employ "examined emotions"; intellectual, emotional, and spiritual curiosity; its necessary companion, doubt; and physical knowledge (what we can learn from, as the gym trainers say, "listening to our bodies"). But a warning: it would be as much a mistake to focus only on experiential knowledge, or creativity and imagination, including knowledge generated by play, as it is to focus only on reason or "hard" science methodologies such as statistics. What is needed in searching for a shared ethics to govern the new technoscience is not a disjunctive approach to our ways of knowing, but a conjunctive one. We need good scientific methodologies (good facts), on the one hand, and space for imagination, creativity, and experiential knowledge (good ethics), on the other. And we need to integrate both into a seamless whole.

It is essential, then, to recognize that all of these ways of knowing must be held in dynamic balance. As important as any one way might be in understanding the ethics of a given situation, any one way of knowing unbalanced by the others is likely to lead us astray. So when I speak of the importance of the imagination in understanding a particular situation, I am not putting down reason, or thereby science.

Before proceeding, a few explanatory words about reason are in order because the nature, worth, and valid role of reason are, collectively, often the focus of strong disagreement in relation to ethics. First, reason can be a concept of uncertain meaning, in that its meaning can vary considerably from one discipline, or even from one person, to another. For instance, lawyers use a narrow definition while philosophers or theologians often use an expansive one.[15] In this book, I use the former. By "reason," I refer strictly to logical, cognitive mentation. This is what theologian Paul Tillich called "technical reason."[16] But Tillich also recognized related but much broader mental processes as reason. By "ontological reason," he referred to a range of such processes, including those that scientists can't quantify. These are what I call "other ways of knowing," and that I distinguish from reason. So we use the same pantheon of intellectual tools but classify them differently.

As significant as the definition of reason, however, are the uses of reason. Although Tillich did not argue against those who use technical reason in the service of limited goals — curing a disease, say, or building a bridge — he did argue against those who use it automatically in the service of all goals. Ontological reason, not technical reason, is what people need when exploring what Tillich called "ultimate concerns" (the universal and existential problems through which humans explore meaning, purpose, identity). Such ultimate concerns are at the heart of ethics. Given both the definition and the use of ontological reason, Tillich would have considered it fundamentally *unreasonable* to assume that people should try to overcome their aesthetic, moral, intuitive, or spiritual proclivities, and *reasonable* to seek guidance from these sources — that is, doing so is part of the use of reason. This corresponds to my overall approach of seeking ethics through all ways of knowing — but, as I say, in this book my references are to reason only in its narrow sense.

What I'm arguing is that there is a difference between what we do mentally in using reason — that is, what the process of reasoning involves — and what we hope to achieve by using it. The narrow definition of reason focuses on the former, the broad one on the latter. Neither definition is wrong, but we can easily cause confusion by not making clear which definition we are using.

Reason and faith are often posited as the two mutually exclusive ways of knowing. Faith is a non-rational (but not irrational) way of knowing. But might they be opposite poles on a spectrum along which the other ways of knowing fall? In that case, some of those other ways of knowing might manifest several characteristics, some of which traditionally would have been seen as falling only within reason and others only within faith. This idea of a continuum, rather than a binary approach, might allow us to find common territory no matter which pole we start from. And, once again, that might help us to find some consensus on ethics.

My own experience has been that some people, in particular many academics, are hostile to ways of knowing other than reason. Might that be self-protective or even self-interested in that while these people may be superior to many others in reasoning ability, they may be inferior to them in other ways of knowing? I wonder, too, if reason might be more easily learned than other ways of knowing? We now know that different parts of the brain are activated when we engage in different activities — for example, when we speak spontaneously as compared to when we read aloud something we have written. I believe that we need to use all parts of our brain to "know" deeply and humanly. I have long hypothesized that our primary decision-making mechanism is often a "gut reaction," not based on reason, but that reason is an essential secondary verification mechanism for such decisions.[17] I note here that priority does not necessarily equate to primacy, so that is not to denigrate reason. Rather, we must listen to all our ways of knowing — including reason — and take into account what each tells us.

The Fifth Building Block: Human Ethics

Some time ago I was asked to speak on the right to health to an international audience at a colloquium on

"AIDS, Health and Human Rights" that was held in France.[18] I proposed that we should start by talking about the universal obligation to respect every person. We should then recognize that one very important way to implement that respect is through the concept of human rights. Starting with the concept of respect for persons, rather than that of human rights, and seeing human rights as one very important way of implementing that respect, helps to avoid the danger of over-legalization that some people argue is inherent in "rights talk" because rights are tools of law. One way to put into practice the principles and values enshrined in human rights is through law, but it is not the only way — or even the principal way, except, perhaps, in Western democracies. Moreover, retaining the use of rights language, but within a broader concept of respect for persons, is likely to counteract arguments that the concept of human rights reflects only the values of one particular cultural and societal reality — a Western one.

Nothing in what I've said is meant to detract from the importance of either human rights or human rights law; rather, I believe that talk of rights is not always the best tool to use for trying to ensure respect for all persons. I do not belong in the camp of philosophers like the French existentialist Jean-Paul Sartre, who wanted to eliminate custom, law, and authority as mediating structures. Sometimes — but, my point is, not always — custom, law, and authority are necessary to finding shared values and a shared ethics. Australian surgeon-philosopher Miles Little provides an interesting insight into this issue. He proposes that we have increasingly "legalized ethics" — we now use law to govern conduct that used to be governed by morality — in order to give ethics the necessary authority, authority that it lacks when it cannot be based on an extrinsic, absolute moral authority such as God or religion, as it was in the past.[19]

I believe that our ethics discourse must also expressly articulate the concept of *human responsibilities*. These are integral to human rights, but often are not articulated as such, for fear of opening up possibilities for the abuse of human rights. The fear is that a state might try to justify a breach of a person's human rights on the grounds that they were not fulfilling their human responsibilities and therefore did not merit respect for their human rights. Respect for human rights should not be dependent on fulfilling our human responsibilities: bad people have the same rights as good.

I also propose that we need to recognize that statements about human rights, including those enshrined in law, are declarative, not constitutive, of respect for persons — for example, we have a right to liberty whether or not anybody says so. Such statements articulate *profound principles of human ethics*. In other words, human rights exist as powerful moral claims, whether or not they are recognized by legal systems. People who are strong advocates of human rights often fail to recognize the dangers inherent in relying always and everywhere on the terminology of rights. Although rights are very powerful tools wherever legal systems recognize them — indeed, the most powerful tool — they are in danger of being totally ignored by societies that are not "rights based." It is important to seek, to the greatest extent possible, implementation of the content of these "rights," even when they are not recognized as legal ones. This is likely to be achieved only if we broaden our terminology and discourse beyond the language of rights (while not abandoning either the terminology or discourse of human rights) to include not only that of human responsibilities, but also that of *human ethics*.

I regard human rights, human responsibilities, and human ethics as interchangeable concepts in that they are alternative ways to achieve the goal they hold in common, that of promoting respect for persons. They can be seen as three alternative doors into the same reality. Which of them is the most appropriate to use as a point of entry in any given situation depends on the situation. Likewise, ethics and law are two sides of the same coin that often overlap when they are each applied to a given issue. Awareness of the wide range of ethical and legal concepts that might apply in a given situation can help us navigate the complex ethical and legal thought needed to address some problems.

The Sixth Building Block: Articulating the Concept of a Shared Ethics

Before looking at how and where we might find a shared ethics, I want to explain in more detail what I mean by this idea. I do not mean that we will have one monolithic, universal ethics. Nor do I mean that we will all just accept one another's ethics — what is called an "ethical pluralism."

Nor do I accept moral relativism — that everyone's views on ethics are as good as anyone else's. Nor do I accept ethical cosmopolitanism, if that means that we must be equally concerned for and equally bonded to everyone.

Humans have evolved over hundreds of thousands of years to bond to special others, such as family and friends or some larger group; some special other living beings, such as pets; and special land, often a country of birth or homeland. We bond more strongly or in a different way inside these parameters than outside them. Ethics must accommodate those realities. Some manifestations of such bonding can be expressed as nepotism, tribalism, patriotism, and nationalism — which can sometimes be reprehensible. But, in fact, the bonds that underlie these manifestations are ethically neutral in themselves. What must be avoided is the unethical, unjust, or evil use of these bonds to cause harm and suffering to others. One barrier to avoiding these harms arises because individuals invest themselves and find their personal identities in these bonds, so challenging them is experienced as a personal attack and destructive of those individuals' identity. We also need to keep in mind that identity always involves seeing how we are both like and unlike others — it unavoidably creates a complex "us" and "them" situation. Such bonding is also the force that forms and animates "identity-based social movements," such as feminism. In the political sphere that translates into identity-based politics. This kind of bonding is an unusual mixture of intense individualism and collectivism, which might explain why it is so hard to oppose the claims made under its umbrella.

One barrier to finding a shared ethics is the metaphysical hunt for "the Truth" — one encompassing truth — that has dominated much of Western and Eastern philosophy.[20] This hunt for Truth currently divides secular from religious societies because we do not agree on what constitutes Truth. Concepts of the secular sacred and a basic presumption in favour of the natural avoid that problem, if we can agree on what they require. That means the language, rhetoric, and symbols employed by future ethicists will need to steer clear of the metaphysical hunt for the Truth, if we are to find a shared base for a shared ethics.

I hasten to point out that abandoning a search for the Truth as a basis for a shared ethics does not mean that we must abandon our own personal belief in that Truth, whatever it might be for us. One way to explain the change I'm suggesting here is that instead of searching for a shared ethics through trying to find agreement as to what constitutes the Truth (an impossible goal in contemporary societies and even more so in a global context), we should search for a shared ethics by finding where we agree in practice (that is, we will have a number of shared truths).

The urban anthropologist Jane Jacobs alerts us to another danger that can occur when we seek a broader-based ethics. The danger occurs in "mixed ethical systems," which need special ethical safeguards. In her book *Systems of Survival*,[21] Jacobs speaks of moral syndromes — the ethical systems governing certain types of activity, whether doing business or running a government, hospital, or university. She proposes that there are two: a guardian moral syndrome (paternalism and its ethics) and a commercial moral syndrome (commercialism and its ethics). Universities and governments are classic examples of the guardian moral syndrome, while industry and business are governed by the commercial moral syndrome. Each system has its own internal ethical safeguards. Problems arise when a mixed moral syndrome, or mixed ethical system, results from a combination of institutions, some of which are governed by the guardian moral syndrome and others by the commercial one.

Jacobs argues that these mixed ethical systems are the most difficult to protect against abuse because the ethics safeguards incorporated into each "moral syndrome" can become inoperative when the syndromes are mixed — they cancel each other out. As a result, we can end up with no ethical safeguards. In a guardian moral syndrome, the guardian must act in the best interests of others, while in a commercial moral syndrome one may act in one's own best interests as long as one acts honestly. Unless the interests that must be given priority in each case happen to coincide, one cannot give priority to both at the same time. Care is needed to avoid the negation of ethics that can occur in mixed systems — for instance, the scandalous behaviour that results when government bureaucrats see their primary role as being entrepreneurs and "doing business," especially to benefit themselves. We should also keep in mind the warning delivered by an old saying in human rights: "Nowhere are human rights more threatened than

when we act purporting to do only good." Our good intentions in such situations — for instance, economic benefit to
our country or scientific advancement — may blind us to
the ethical risks and harms involved.

In seeking common ground in ethics, we also need to
be careful that we do not compromise important values.
Sometimes there is no common or middle ground; moreover, common and middle grounds are not necessarily
the same. For instance, one must be either for or against
legalizing euthanasia — there is no middle position, nor
is there a common one, on that issue. Alternatively, sometimes we can agree on what should be the outcome in a
particular case, but we don't agree on the reasons for
adopting that stance. For example, many feminists and
many religious people are against surrogate motherhood,
but for very different reasons. Feminists see it as degrad-
ing women, religious people as denigrating human
procreation and harming children. There is common
ground that surrogate motherhood is morally wrong and
on the outcome that it should be banned, but not on the
reasons for supporting that moral judgement or outcome.
In short, we can agree, although for different reasons.

This means that we must look at the reasons behind a
decision, not just the decision itself, to see the precedent
that decision sets for future cases. Although two different
lines of reasoning can result in the same decision in one
case, they may result in very different outcomes in
another case. For instance, one group could justify the
withdrawal of life-support treatment to allow a person to
die because the burdens of the treatment outweigh any

benefits; another could see the withdrawal as passive euthanasia and approve of it on that ground. In a future case, withdrawal might not be justified after a burden/benefit assessment, but those who advocate for the wider availability of euthanasia could argue that the previous case sets a precedent supporting euthanasia and, hence, supports giving lethal injections.

So, how can we seek a broad-based shared ethics and still avoid compromising our core values and accommodate the conflicts that cannot be resolved? Perhaps the answer is to be found in a "mosaic of sharing" or partly overlapping consensuses,[22] which together make up a complex multicoloured tapestry or carpet. In other words, I see a difference between a shared ethics (with each group we can find some values we share) and a universal ethics (we all agree on the same values). In a shared ethics, we would find consensus on some matters with some people or groups, and on other matters with other people or groups. I'm assuming that our consensus represents a genuine commitment to those matters and is not just indifference or simply disengaged tolerance with respect to them. The fact that there are some values, concepts, or ideas that we share would create a different tone for discussion of those on which we disagree — perhaps in some instances we would see these disagreements as less divisive. At present, we focus only on our disagreements, especially in media reporting. This is not neutral in its impact. Imagine a family that focused only on its disagreements. It would be astonishing if such a family survived intact. We need to create a general climate of agreement about what ethics requires in given circumstances, but our climate must also accommodate disagreements as the exception. At present, we have a general climate of disagreement, with agreement as the exception. I am proposing we start our "ethics talk" from where we agree and move to our disagreements rather than vice versa. This change may seem inconsequential, but it can have major impact. We have seen that in the relation between law and ethics. Starting from law means law informs ethics; starting from ethics that ethics informs law. The outcome can be radically different.

In order to start from consensus, not disagreement, we might need to agree on three things: that we should seek to identify the values on which we agree that fall in a shared middle range between the poles at each extreme, a process that must be understood as excluding unethical compromises; that the search is a continuous process; and that it involves ways of knowing that include, but are not limited, to, reason — for instance, that we require imagination as well. We can then identify how broad the middle is — that is, we would accept that there are matters at either end of the spectrum of values that are not acceptable to all and that we will never agree upon, but we hope we would also discover there is much that all of us can accept. I am proposing a thick overlap of borders concept — that we might start from different poles, but there is a big (one hopes) overlap of common territory in the middle, in which we all are, in fact, "at home."

My concept of a shared ethics can be most easily explained, perhaps, by another metaphor: Imagine building a hotel. The ground floor must be open to everyone and large enough to accommodate all who want to enter. The second floor might have some special facilities where only certain groups of people want to go. Upper floors might have private rooms that are each decorated differently according to the occupants' personal preferences. The ground floor is the shared ethics; the second floor might be different cultural, national, or religious practices or beliefs; the upper floors are smaller groups such as families or individuals. For the structure to be viable, it must have a ground floor strong enough to support the entire building; that ground floor must be open to everyone; people must reach their communal or private rooms by way of the ground floor; and what they do on those upper floors must not threaten the structural integrity of the hotel as a whole.

Now the crucial question is, Can we truly find a shared ethics for a globalized world? As I explained earlier, we cannot any longer rely on a shared religion to provide our shared ethical base. But might we be able to find some universals that are common to all people whether or not they are religious and, if so, no matter what religion they espouse? Might we able to say that these universals are so widely shared over such a long period of time across so many different cultures that they can be taken as characteristics of being human — that is, they are innate to being human?

The danger in that approach is that some of our worst characteristics, as well as our best, are innate to being human. Can we deal with that danger by using a concept of maintaining and promoting human good as a touch-stone for a shared base? That concept might include: Respect for individuals and their relationships to others — intimates and strangers — and for all life. Respect for community and its maintenance. Recognition of a shared desire to fully live fully human lives. Acknowledgement of obligations to fulfill certain physical and non-physical needs of others. Respect for freedom. And not harming the deep human need to experience creativity, imagina-tion, and play. Might the search for meaning be the most fundamental characteristic of humanness? Could that be a manifestation of an innate moral element in humans as individuals and collectives that we can use to found a base against which we can test the rightness or wrong-ness of what we do? We can't prove there is such an element — but, when we can't be certain either way, we are better off assuming that there is than that there is not.

The central question is this: How can we hold in cre-ative tension what seems at first to be an impossible combination? We need an ethics that will safeguard indi-vidual rights and liberties but also protect the community; that emphasizes justice and redress for wrongs but also compassion, mercy, forgiveness, and love; and that is based on norms that are acceptable to individuals but also shared across time and place.

It's likely that much of what we find we share ethi-cally comes from some earlier cultural source we have in common. But new genetic knowledge is also causing us to ask whether there might also be some shared biological base for human morality and ethics. The fact that humans are "moral animals"[23] — that across widely varying cultures, times, and different types and sizes of societies, humans have employed a concept of morality — makes this likely. If we eventually prove the existence of genes that make us "moral animals" — just as it has been shown that nurturing behaviour in rats depends on genes[24] — such genes may have to be activated by environmental triggers during certain critical window periods of time, failing which they shut down. It is essential that I explain more fully what I mean here.

As I have emphasized, I reject genetic reductionism — that we are nothing more than "gene machines," that everything about us is simply an expression of our genes, even our moral and ethical sensibilities. Rather, if such genes exist, they are one tool among many that allow us to implement our moral and ethical capacities to govern our behaviour. One way to describe what I mean is to compare these genes (if they exist) with a radio. Radios allow us to hear programs put to air, but they do not determine those programs' content. Likewise, assuming that genes giving us the capacity to be moral exist, they do not determine the content of our behaviour — rather, they provide us with the capacity to judge it morally. We are free to decide how we exercise that capacity, and what we see as ethical or unethical conduct as a result.

This discussion leads to another interesting question: Might the new science help us to find a shared base from which to launch our search for a shared ethics? The possibility of new science helping to solve ethical problems provides a nice contrast to the situation with which we are much more familiar — new science creating new ethical problems. How might science help? One example is provided by brain scans taken with magnetic resonance imaging machines. They demonstrate that the brain is much more active when a person is telling a lie than when they are telling the truth. Scientists interpret this as meaning that the basic state of the human mind is to tell the truth.[25] Could we argue that such basic states are an inherent shared human characteristic, and therefore might be examples of a shared substrate on which morality can develop? If so, we might be able to agree that lying is inherently wrong, although we might also agree an exception can sometimes be excused or, more rarely, justified.

The Seventh Building Block: Basic Presumptions

Basic presumptions are the foundation stones from which we start an ethical analysis, or any other analysis or decision-making process. They establish the ethical foundation or starting point on which we build our arguments. We cannot avoid such a starting point. And we usually take whatever basic presumption we use to ground our ethics analysis and decision-making as a given, as self-evident. But in fact, there is a choice to be made, and that choice has a far from neutral effect on our ethical analysis and, consequently, our decisions. The famous Artic explorer John Franklin showed that he understood the impact and importance of basic presumptions when venturing into the unknown physical world with his advice: "[I]n navigation one must fix one's starting-position as precisely as one's objective."[26]

In ethics, there are four basic presumptions: *No*: we must not do this; *Yes*: there are no restrictions or conditions on what we want to do; *No, unless . . .* : no, we must not do it unless we can justify it, and these are the requirements for justification; and *Yes, but . . .* : yes, we may do it, but not if certain circumstances prevail. Most ethical analysis involves situations where we must choose to use either a *no, unless* or a *yes, but* analysis. You might think that it doesn't matter which of those we favour, and that is true where the ethical answer is relatively clear. But where we are equally doubtful about which of two courses of action to take, these two presumptions give polar opposite results. In such situations, a *no, unless* presumption means we may not proceed — a good example of this approach is the precautionary principle used in environmental ethics, which requires those creating risks to the environment to show that it is reasonably safe to do so before proceeding. In contrast, a *yes, but* presumption in the same circumstances means we may proceed until it becomes obvious that it is not reasonably safe to do so.

One particular use of basic presumptions in practice merits special emphasis here. There is a radical difference between starting from ethical principles and analysis and seeing what that would allow or prohibit ethically regarding a given technology, and starting from the technology and seeking an ethics to "fit" it in order to allow its development and use. In the former case, ethics informs our use of the technology; in the latter, the technology informs our ethics. The conclusions about ethics are unlikely to be the same.

The Eighth Building Block:
The Source and Nature of Ethics

There are three main stances concerning the source of ethics. The source of morality or ethics can be seen as entirely extrinsic to humans; or as having some features that are extrinsic and some that are intrinsic to humans, that is, as having a mixed extrinsic-intrinsic source; or as completely intrinsic to humans.

Principle-based ethicists believe there is a principled base against which one tests the validity of decisions about ethics. Traditionally, that base was supernatural — a Supreme Being, God, or His human representatives such as an absolute religious or moral authority or an absolute monarch — and it still is for those whose ethics stem from their religious beliefs. The basis of morality for people who are of this view is usually religious — although it can be simply spiritual. This is a "pure" extrinsic-to-humans view of the source of morality and ethics.

Some principle-based ethicists see morality as an effort by humans to fulfill our intrinsic need to bring ourselves into line with the extrinsic will or larger plan of a Supernatural Being, or God. This is a mixed extrinsic-intrinsic view of the source of morality and ethics.

For some other principle-based ethicists, the source of ethics can be found in nature or the natural order —some followers of Natural Law take this approach. These principle-based ethicists believe that searching for ethics is simply being human, and that this search can be seen as part of our larger search for the laws of nature — just as we search for natural physical laws in science, we search for natural moral laws in ethics. Seeking to align ourselves with those moral laws may be part of our effort to fulfill our yearning to live in harmony with the universe — an effort and yearning that is a characteristic of being human. This is a "pure" intrinsic-to-humans view of the source of morality and ethics.

In summary, principle-based ethicists can appeal to a purely extrinsic source for the basis of their morality — that is, God or the Natural Order. Or to a mixed extrinsic-intrinsic source: God made humans to seek morality, and therefore God is the extrinsic source of the intrinsic source of morality within humans. Or to a purely intrinsic source: morality is part of shared human nature and its content is not determined simply by the preferences of the individual person.

Some utilitarian philosophers, such as the German Jürgen Habermas, also believe that searching for morality — and applying it through ethics — is intrinsic to being human. In other words, they see the search for morality as having an intrinsic source — it is to be found in humans as part of their intrinsic nature — but they do not attribute the fact that we have an intrinsic need to undertake a search for morality to any external or supernatural source. Many, and probably most, contemporary utilitarians do not accept God as the primary source of societal ethics, even if they are religious and they base their personal morality on religion. Habermas speaks of deep human intuitions as to what is right or wrong and describes these as constituting an "ethics of the [human] species."[27] That view is one that can also found a princi-ple-based ethics. In short, some principle-based ethicists and these utilitarians have some overlap in their concepts of the source and nature of ethics.

All of the people who fit into the two categories described above can be contrasted with the third group — the moral relativist utilitarians. They see morality and ethics as something with no natural roots — whether in human nature, Nature, or the supernatural — but as something created by humans in order to avoid harm and suffering for individuals or society, and to promote "good." For them, ethics is the outcome of the practical decision-making of any person or group with the power to have their moral and ethical preferences prevail in any given situation. They do not acknowledge that ethics has a substantive base (whether extrinsic or intrinsic to the human person) against which a given decision can be judged. Rather, what is or is not ethical simply "depends on all the circumstances." That can make ethics, at best, just a matter of right ethical process — that is, if the process used for reaching an ethical decision is ethical (the decision-maker is without conflict of interest, all peo-ple affected by the decision are heard, and so on), the decision can be assumed to be ethical. Note, however, that while, in theory, relativists argue it is impossible to find objective truth, inconsistently, they often conclude that "their ethical truth," as they see it, is better than their "opponents' ethical truth."

The adherents of this pragmatic utilitarian approach point out that once you abandon the idea of grounding ethics in the absolute, you abandon the metaphysical hunt for truth and open the field to a more genuine, humble, and open form of dialogue through which you can reach ethical conclusions. Adherents of this view argue such conclusions are more likely to generate a wider consensus and are also more likely to be implemented than those that are perceived to be imposed.

One danger of this approach is that ethics can become simply a matter of personal preferences and individual — or sometimes identity-based group — decision-making. And, because its existence depends only on us, we can choose whether ethics should exist — that is, one possible response is ethical nihilism. So, for example, a decision-maker could decide that no ethical requirements should be applied by society to limit the use of new reproductive technologies. Moreover, this approach makes it more difficult to justify implementing ethical requirements at the institutional or societal level, especially when doing so is perceived as a source of power and control by those to whom the requirements apply. A common response is that "what I want to do is nobody else's business, and certainly not that of some ethics body whose ethical judgements are no better than mine."

A moral relativist approach to ethics also makes — or at least it *should* make — the ethics of the decision-maker a matter of great importance. And, paradoxically, that leads to recognizing a need for virtues ethics — that those deciding on ethics should be moral people — which is also a feature of deontological ethics. So the principle-based ethicists can agree with this group of utilitarians on the need for ethical decision-makers — a principle that all other utilitarians would also accept. The difference, however, is that deontological ethics has safeguards that are independent of the decision-makers — namely, its basic principles — in case the decision-makers are not virtuous or moral people; and those principles also act as a guide for the decision-makers whether or not they are virtuous. Ironically, that analysis constitutes a utilitarian defence of principle-based ethics, which is not a contradiction.

Another way to examine the differences between these groups of ethicists is through the lens of the following question: In whose hands is "ethics power" placed? Where that power is placed depends on what each group views as the source of ethics. The principle-based ethicists — the deontologists — place "ethics power" in their principles and the external source of those principles, although human agents must exercise that power, which means their decisions still need safeguarding. The intrinsic "human-based morality" ethicists — who are usually called "principle-based utilitarians" — place power in the collective human psyche as expressed in moral consensus, but likewise we must always question whether that is operating ethically and being interpreted and applied ethically in any given circumstance. And the procedural-based ethicists — the moral relativist utilitarians — do not see ethics as having any extrinsic or intrinsic substantive base, which means what is ethical is determined by who has the power to impose their ethical beliefs in any given circumstance.

I think we have the best chance to find broadly shared ethics between principle-based ethicists and human-based-morality utilitarians. We need to identify and promote the ethics overlap between them and the shared ethics that emerge as a result. In the next chapter, I propose that linking the secular and the sacred, by adopting a concept of the secular sacred, can unite these ethicists and everyone else who accepts that some things are sacred, whether they see the sacred's source as religious or purely natural or secular.

The concept of the secular sacred is one of a group of closely related concepts that I explore in this book, concepts that we can use to help guide our ethical imaginations. The others include: *a basic presumption in favour of the natural; whether truth is a friend or foe in finding a shared ethics; respect for all life, in particular human life; respect for intrinsic human dignity;* and *respect for the human spirit.* My hope is that these concepts might help us to bridge the differences between us on matters of ethics and, in so doing, help us to find a shared ethics. The survival of the world of the future, at least as the kind of world most of us would want to live in, may well depend on our success in achieving that goal.

II

A POETRY OF ETHICS:
CREATING A LANGUAGE OF THE ETHICAL IMAGINATION

FINDING A POETRY OF ETHICS:
THE SECULAR SACRED

I INTRODUCED THE concept of the *secular sacred* in my book *The Ethical Canary*. It was more or less a throwaway line, added as the book was about to go to press, but over time it has come to play a major role in my thinking about ethical issues.

I propose that linking the secular and the sacred is one key to finding a shared ethics. Those whose source of ethics is God or God-Nature (God and His creation, including humans) will have a concept of the religious-spiritual sacred and accept that certain moral and ethical principles flow from that. Those whose source of ethics is innate human morality have a concept of the secular sacred (for instance, they will accept that certain aspects of life are sacrosanct; not everything that could be done to life, in particular, human life, may ethically be done to it) and certain moral and ethical principles that should be respected and should govern our conduct flow from that. What the two have in common is a concept of the sacred. And where the two coincide is where the religious sacred and secular sacred overlap — the substantive content of that overlap can form the basis for a shared ethics. Both approaches contrast with one that rejects religion and any other external moral authority, as well as any moral base intrinsic to humans; consequently, this approach employs no concept of the sacred.

In order to examine more closely the concept of the secular sacred, let's begin by looking at what might be necessary features of one part of that term — the sacred. First, that which we consider sacred must have some kind of authenticity apart from utility, personal preference, or a desire that it be such — it must have "a life of its own." I recognize that "authenticity" is a philosophically loaded concept, and that what constitutes authenticity is much disputed. Here I simply leave open what that might be. My point is that "something more" — some intrinsic characteristics, which may be symbolic — is required to constitute the sacred.

For those who are religious, the authenticity of the sacred is determined by God and by God's will as to how we should act toward God and God's creation — other humans, other animals, all forms of life, the natural world. I recognize that what is regarded as sacred by religions can be culture specific, and that the degree to which the sacred is associated with either numinous or everyday experiences varies greatly across cultures and religions. But the important point is that all cultures and religions have a sense of the sacred, even if some might not characterize it as such and although its content varies greatly from one to the other. The commonality is that the sacred is special, in its most generic sense, and the profane (the non-sacred) ordinary.

For people who are not religious in the orthodox sense, the authentically sacred, in the form of the secular sacred, can be found in the essence of being human — the search for morality, exercising the power to become fully oneself, undertaking the search for meaning in life. The authentically sacred might also be experienced, and as a result identified, in a sense of wonder and awe.

The sacred, then, requires that we respect the integrity of the elements that allow us to fully experience being fully human; in doing so, we protect that experience. Likewise, an element of being fully human is to experience the sacred. This circularity brings to mind, once again, the mythical image of the snake swallowing its tail that I referred to before. It is probably no accident that it so often seems appropriate to use this image to explain some aspect of what is involved in "doing ethics." There is often a circularity, not a linear progression from one point to another, in our search for ethics — "what goes around comes around." We need to experience awe and wonder to access a sense of the sacred; but, in turn, that sense can be the doorway to awe and wonder.

Beyond the question, What are the elements of the sacred? we must now ask, What is the goal of promoting a sense of the secular sacred?

I see the concept of the secular sacred as a companion to the idea of a basic presumption in favour of the natural, an idea that I'll explore later. The concepts are related in that both can help us to find a shared base for a shared ethics. I'm differentiating here between a shared *base* for a shared ethics, and a shared ethics. We need both. The difference is that the former includes procedural principles on which we can agree — such as a presumption in favour of the natural. But even though we agree on that, we might not agree on what that presumption requires from us, ethically, in a given situation. That is, we might have a shared ethical base but still not find a shared ethics on that issue.

In talking about the secular sacred, I propose that the sacred is not only a concept that applies in a religious or ritualized context, but also one that operates at a general societal — or secular — level. I'm proposing it as a concept that encapsulates an experience that we might use to help people find their most authentic individual selves. This is not to endorse intense individualism; indeed, my intent is the opposite. I believe our most authentic selves are to be found in the complex interaction of knowing ourselves, relating to others, appreciating our place in the great web of all life, and seeing ourselves as part of the earth, the stars, the universe, and the cosmos. Some scientists tell us that we came from stardust — that the earliest form of life on earth might have arrived in meteorites that crashed; to rephrase the Ash Wednesday liturgy, "Remember man thou art stardust and unto stardust thou shalt return." That fact, assuming that it will prove to be correct, and the idea that science can verify it, is astonishing and wondrous. The acute and continuous awareness of a mind-blowing web of relationships — that is what I call the human spirit. The sacred is rightly enlisted when it will protect and promote that spirit, and wrongly used when it will do harm to it.

In promoting a concept of the secular sacred, we need to acknowledge that the concept of the *traditional sacred* has been abused and caused serious harm as a result. While it sometimes protected against certain practices in war, it has also been misused in the cause of war and violence, as in the Christian Crusades to protect sacred places and in the Islamic use of religious concepts such as holy jihad to justify terrorism. Like all powerful ideas, the sacred has the potential to be used for both good and evil.

The sacred is a concept that we should use to protect that which is most precious in human life, starting with life itself. I am suggesting that, in contemporary secular societies, the sacred can still function and can best do so through the idea of the secular sacred. Although our Western societies do not use religion as the direct basis for public policy, we still need to have access to a concept of the sacred, in particular to maintain respect for all life, especially human life, and to find shared values promoting that respect. The term *sanctity of life*[1] is often associated with the sacred. This phrase has taken on political connotations, however, and is often misunderstood and misused. As a result it is confusing — so I will not use it here. Nonetheless, today — whether or not we are religious — we have more need than ever for the respect for life it was meant to implement. Adopting the idea of the secular sacred gives us the conceptual tool we need to protect that which we hold most precious, in particular, life.

Already we can find examples of the secular sacred in our societies — sometimes in the form of "sacred cows." Medicare — the Canadian publicly funded health-care system — is often described as such. The "sacred value" Medicare establishes is that we are all equal, especially when we are sick and need care. Medicare is seen by Canadians as establishing and affirming one of our most important shared societal values — namely, that we care for one another, especially when we are in need and vulnerable.

It may seem selfish of us to be worrying about experiencing the sacred in our own lives when there are millions of people in the world facing war and natural tragedies and starvation, without clean water to drink and without shelter, who have no access to even the most basic medical care and whose children die in hundreds of thousands each year. What about the secular sacred in their lives? How can we speak of the secular sacred in our lives when we turn a blind eye to tragedies such as those Stephen Lewis described in last year's Massey Lectures, *Race Against Time*[2], arising out of the spread of HIV/AIDS in Africa? To do so seems like the ultimate hypocrisy, and in some ways, it is. But I propose we might also respond to such tragedies as a society more adequately and ethically if we have a sense of the secular sacred. And having that sense requires us to recognize and talk about it.

Experiencing the Sacred

How, then, do we experience the sacred in our secular societies?

What we regard as sacred is often associated with that which elicits feelings of awe and wonder, that primordial sense of amazement I've mentioned before. Many people experience that feeling on first seeing their newborn baby. We can also experience it in our everyday lives when we watch a magnificent sunset, hear the birds' dawn chorus, or hold a newborn kitten or puppy; see two foxes wandering in the moonlight, along a grassy treed slope, beside a busy downtown expressway, or gaze at a pair of blue herons flying home at sunset high over a great river; are surrounded by beautiful music or art; feel an intimate bond with another human; or have the intricacies and order of the universe revealed to us by science. A sense of the sacred is present when we feel awe at being alive and conscious of the beauty, world, and life around us. It is no accident that we often find that experience in nature — in perceiving the exquisite minuteness of a tiny flower or insect, or in being lost in the grandiosity of wilderness and vast night skies. Indeed, one place where we might find the secular sacred operating is in the environmental protection movement, some aspects of which mirror those of a religion. The movement functions through shared "truths" and ideology, and the bonding that results from sharing those beliefs; it causes people to focus on a reality external to themselves; it provides an opportunity for transcendence — belonging to and protecting something larger than oneself; its adherents demonstrate a willingness to make sacrifices and to suffer to promote the great cause they believe in; and they are concerned for future generations, handing on their values and beliefs to their descendants. Religious Studies scholars Paul Nathanson and Katherine Young have proposed that such movements are secular religions. If we can have a secular religion, it would seem logical that we can also have a secular sacred.

One question all this raises is what constitutes the difference between a purely emotional or aesthetic experience and a sacred one? In passing, I would say that no experience of the sacred is focused entirely on the edification of *self*; it always has to do with relations with others, whether in the natural or supernatural world. Perhaps one distinction between an aesthetic and a sacred experience is that the aesthetic relates us to ourselves, the sacred to some "other." The sacred has a goal of transformation and, therefore, leads to new forms of behaviour in relation to the social order, the natural order, or, for some, the divine order.

In our secular societies, we may confuse religion with religious experiences, and those of us who have abandoned the former may mistakenly believe we have also abandoned the latter. But religious experiences are primordial and universal in humans — they are part of the essence of being human. Indeed, as I suggested previously, they might be hard-wired into our DNA — a suggestion that is controversial in a couple of ways. Those who are religious object that it opens up *genetic reductionism* — the idea that we are nothing more than the expression of our genes, and that religious belief is nothing more than such a genetic expression. Meanwhile, those people who reject religion deny that religious experience might be an integral element of the larger human experience, intrinsic to being human.

The companion experiences to awe and wonder (the sacred) are fear and trembling (the taboo). A secular society also still needs the concept of a taboo: a taboo protects that which we hold most dear, that which we hold sacred. In other words, the taboo and the sacred are two sides of the same coin. and we need secular concepts of both in searching for a shared ethics.

Fear and trembling have been wrongfully used by some people to control others, often in the name of religion, and we have rightly condemned and sought to prevent that abuse. But in throwing out fear and trembling, we may also throw out awe and wonder — and that's a mistake. Fear can be destructive (pathological fear), but it can also be protective (healthy fear). We need healthy fear to protect our individual physical being and also our collective metaphysical being — our values, ethics, and shared morality, which are important elements of what can be called society's psyche. Moreover, we need to have a healthy fear for the well-being of future generations if we are to hold the future on trust for them. To take a lesson from First Nations people, in formulating ethical questions we would do well to ask: What does looking back seven generations teach us about the issues we face? What does looking forward seven generations warn us about those issues? And what impact might our planned action — for example, to alter our children's genes or to legalize euthanasia — have on our descendants seven generations from now?

Asked another way, what are our present ethical obligations to future generations? What must we regard as sacred and hold on trust for them in order not to leave them worse off than we are or with less choices or options than we have? What do we owe them? What does an ethics of responsibility — as compared with an ethics of rights — require of us? The entities that need to be seen as secular sacred and held on trust must extend beyond physical realities to include important metaphysical realities, in particular, important shared societal values such as respect for all life.

In short, we still need taboos, and we still need the taboo's companion concept, that of the sacred. We have, however, lost access to both concepts in determining the ethics of much of our conduct in our contemporary world. I propose we urgently need to rediscover these concepts if we are to make ethical decisions about, for example, new reproductive technologies (NRTs). And we also need to find them in order to act ethically in the face of horrible new possibilities opened up by the life sciences — for instance, those of bioterrorism — if we are to ensure that the life sciences do not become "death sciences" in the hands of terrorists.[3] Concepts of the secular sacred and the secular taboo will not be sufficient to ensure that such abuse does not occur, but they will help us determine how to think and act ethically.

I wrote earlier about my belief in the importance of moral intuition as a way of knowing about ethics. Now I add this further consideration. Might a sense of the sacred be necessary to maintaining our capacity for moral intuition? Just as our muscles deteriorate if we don't engage in physical exercise, it seems reasonable to assume that our other capacities, such as moral intuition or capacity for compassion, might deteriorate if not used regularly. We know that failure to be sensitive to ethical issues in an institution, company, or workplace makes future failures more likely — it creates a low "ethical tone" — and the contrary is true when there is sensitivity to ethical issues. Perhaps we could regard regular recognition of the secular sacred as yoga for our moral intuition; vice versa, practicing compassion, for instance, might allow us to experience the sacred.

Describing the Sacred

Assuming that a secular sacred is possible — that is, that the sacred can exist outside the context of religion — how do we recognize and describe it? Can anything be sacred (for example, can money be sacred?) or must the sacred have certain inherent characteristics? Is what we recognize as sacred merely a matter of choice, or is there some inherent reality or characteristic to the sacred?

We already see some things as priceless; we hold that they must not or cannot be bought and sold. In a well-known advertisement for a credit card, love, fun, and tenderness are portrayed as realities that cannot be bought and sold, whereas, we are told, "For everything else there is MasterCard." Is the contemporary sacred that which must not be commodified, must not be bought and sold? Such a proposition leads us once again to the split between principle-based approaches to ethics and utilitarian and relativist approaches. Principle-based ethicists would say some things are absolutely sacred and therefore must not be available for sale — the human body and its parts, especially gametes (sperm and ova). Moral relativists — if they agreed to contemplate the sacred at all — would take the opposite approach: they would say determining the sacred (if sacred in this context means that which must not be available for sale) depends on the balance of risks, harms, and benefits of allowing or prohibiting commercialization.

Another way to investigate the sacred is to explore what it is meant to protect, if anything. Might our metaphyisical reality, such as important shared values, be such an entity? For instance, parents' and children's bonds to one another — especially parents' unconditional love for their children simply *because* they are their children — are often described as sacred.

Sacredness may also protect our physical reality, in particular that of our own bodies, and that of the world around us, or what I will refer to as nature. In the chapters that follow, I discuss some of the radical ideas for using new technologies on the human embryo and human body, and interventions that are now possible or proposed. The progression of science's ability to change the human body has been breathtakingly fast, starting with transplants and cosmetic surgery and moving on to creating chimeras (human-animal combinations) and cyborgs (human-machine combinations). For the people who promote and laud such developments, the natural essence of being human has no element of the sacred, and therefore contains nothing that must be protected and preserved through restricting what we can do in light of what we ought not to do in order to maintain the integrity of our humanness. One expression of this view — one that now seems relatively mild (from a physical perspective) in light of developments since it was first expressed — is that humans are no different in any essential moral respect from other animals. Such views are articulated in philosophical propositions such as Princeton philosopher Peter Singer's "speciesism." This concept holds that it is wrongful discrimination to favour humans, just because they are human, over other animals. At least speciesism is a concept that still entails respect for the natural realm of life. Rodney Brooks in his book *Flesh and Machines*[4] goes further. He argues that humans are not special, and are not superior to machines with artificial intelligence (AI) and robots; in fact, we may be inferior in some respects. Such views are accompanied by the loss of any concept of the sacredness of being human or human beings.[5]

In addition to protecting our bodies, a sense of the sacred may also protect the physical world around us. The importance of having a basic presumption in favour of respect for nature and the natural when we search for a shared ethics is something I discuss later. Here, it is relevant to note that nature and the sacred have been closely associated throughout human history. We can see nature as an aspect of the sacred, and we can also experience the sacred through contact with nature; that is, nature can be a vehicle for the sacred. Soil, soul, and society are inter-twined and complementary. Soil represents a reverential relationship with the natural earth, animals, and plants. Soul is the essential quality of everything — life, air, water, friendship, and so on. And society is our collective cultural reality and identity.

I believe it is important that we see ourselves as part of nature, and at the same time to avoid an anthropocentric view of it. Nature is not here merely for humans to manipulate or for human benefit. It's not just an obstacle to be overcome. It has inherent worth. Recognizing the truth of this may be one manifestation of the belief that nature is sacred. Seeing nature as sacred protects it.

We need to understand the nature of nature and its role in our lives and in how we find meaning. We seem to have forgotten the importance of the wild and of the experience of it to the human spirit. Reminding ourselves of that would be a first essential step in appreciating the content of our obligation to preserve it. Seeing wilderness and animal species (what we call nature) as sacred and thereby affirming that they have worth in their own right (a non-anthropocentric view), not just because they are of value and benefit to humans (an anthropocentric view), can shift our thinking about our ethical obligation towards them. Indeed, such a view shifts the focus of our analyses from our rights as humans to our responsibili-ties. It can promote a shift from a culture of entitlement to a culture of responsibility. Making that shift is crucial to our own protection, and the protection of nature, far into the future.

The Secular Sacred and the Role of Ritual

It is probably a mistake to see the secular and the sacred as being opposites. Rather, the "pure secular" and the "pure sacred" are opposite poles of a continuum, and the secular sacred is comprised of various degrees of each. For example, in order not to offend its sacredness, Balinese temple dance was intentionally altered to be profane before it was performed as entertainment outside the temple. But the form of dance that developed as entertainment was so beautiful it was taken back into the temple, at which point it again became sacred. The nature of any conduct, its purpose, and the setting in which it takes place are relevant when determining whether something is purely secular or purely sacred or secular sacred. Moreover, one person witnessing a dance in a temple could experience it as secular, another as sacred, and another as secular sacred depending on the beliefs of each person. All of this, taken together, tells us that the sacred has intrinsic and subjective elements as well as extrinsic and objective ones, and might well require the presence of all of these to be seen and experienced as authentic.

Humans have long used rituals as a bridge from the secular to the sacred in order to establish and experience the sacred. But what is the relationship of ritual to the secular sacred? I suggest that it is the bridge that connects secular to sacred. Perhaps rituals in secular activities such as sport or gastronomy might provide some insight in this regard.

Ritual is an outward sign of an invisible reality. For instance, sports rituals allow us to experience invisible bonding with other fans cheering for "our" team. I believe that as a society we've lost a sense of the sacred because we've lost so many opportunities to participate collectively in ritual and thereby experience respect, reverence, and transcendence, the traditional tools for establishing and experiencing the sacred. The solution is not to practice ritual alone, however. Although the search for meaning can be both individual and collective, the use of ritual must be collective or it risks becoming an obsessive-compulsive disorder. But even when we live in families, we have lost access to ritual. Witness the decline of something as common as the family dinner. Many of us no longer see food as sacred in any way, its preparation and sharing as involving ritual, and meals as settings for communication, especially for the family. Might a sense of the secular sacred help us to better understand what we have lost and how we might regain it, in particular through revitalizing rituals that can provide the connections we need to experience and nurture the human spirit collectively?

Daniel Yankelovich, who surveys current values of Americans and how they change, has found that the fastest-growing trend was a longing to belong to something larger than oneself, a longing for transcendence.[6] Transcendence might require a sense of the sacred, even if it's only just the secular sacred. The novelist Carol Shields puts the following question into the mouth of one of her famous characters, Larry, a middle-aged Canadian: "[W]hat will happen to a world that's lost its connection with the sacred? We long for ecstasy, to stand outside of the self in order to transcend that self, but how do we get there?"[7] The traditional path was from religion to the sacred to ecstasy to transcendence. Can we experience transcendence if one or more of these steps are left out? Although I know that not everyone will agree, I believe that achieving transcendence is important, because from transcendence (the feeling of belonging to something larger than oneself) we move to transformation — fully becoming our authentic selves. In other words, transcendence (and longing for it) and transformation (which is only possible through transcendence) are linked. I speak more about how we might "fully become our authentic selves" in a later chapter.

As a final point in my discussion of the secular sacred, I should point out that in arguing for adopting it as a tool to help us find a shared ethics, I am not in any way meaning to diminish the importance of the *religious sacred* to those who hold such beliefs. Moreover, even though we will not all hold the same beliefs as to what is sacred and what is not because of our different religions, the fact that we believe in the sacred is itself an important bond among religious people. I believe the secular sacred could become such a bond between those who are religious and those who are not, as well as between non-religious people with different beliefs, assuming we accept the concept.

Now I want to turn to the topic of the importance of language in finding and doing ethics. One link between the sacred and ethics is that both are mediated, at least in part, through words, often in the form of poetry or poetic language. Poetry is the language of the human spirit, the language through which we have access to the inchoate worlds we must enter to fully experience our humanness. Poetry comes into existence when the words of a poet create the music of a poem. Hearing both the words and their music can give us access to the ways of knowing, in addition to reason, that we need to use in ethics. In particular, poetry is the major language of the imagination. So let's now have a closer look at the links between poetry and the language of ethics, and see how these links might help us to find a shared ethics.

FINDING A POETRY OF ETHICS: THE IMPORTANCE OF LANGUAGE

Words matter. Language is never neutral in ethics. Our choice of it involves *danger* and *opportunity* — two words that in combination mean "crisis" in Mandarin Chinese. And in many ways, choosing our language is one of our greatest challenges in searching for shared ethics in a global world. It can attract or repel, reveal or conceal, calm or anger, give or take power, create or destroy trust.

I have long thought that we will find a shared ethics through the language of poetry, not rationality. This does not mean that reason is irrelevant to the search for a shared ethics or that the ethics we find will be irrational — although it might well be non-rational, that is, based on ways of knowing other than reason. In other words, as I have emphasized many times, all our human ways of knowing are needed in the search for a shared ethics. I believe the language of poetry is the way in which we can best have access to many of these ways of knowing. We need a language of moral imagination and moral intuition because it is primarily through imagination and intuition that we can deepen the understanding we require to make decisions on ethical matters. Reason is also an essential way of knowing, but as I've noted, often functions as a verification mechanism to make sure our other ways of knowing have not led us astray.

Language can be used to create walls and to demolish them, whether those walls are literal or metaphorical, sometimes just by making us aware of their presence and impact. The Soweto poet Oswald Mtshali's poem "Walls" raises such awareness and anticipates what is needed to demolish the walls he describes.

Walls
Man is
a great wall builder
The Berlin Wall
The Wailing Wall of Jerusalem
But the wall
most impregnable
Has a moat
flowing with fright
around his heart
A wall without windows
for the spirit to breeze through
A wall
without a door
for love to walk in.

In the past, the arts — including poetry — were closely entwined with religion. The great religious texts relied on poetry because, like all true art, poetry gives us access to metaphysical and spiritual realities. Just as the molecules that make up a genome, when organized in particular ways, come to life as each living being, so poetry gives life to words: Words are the nucleotides; metaphors and analogies the genes; the images and insights they "code for" the proteins; the composite entity of thoughts and feelings the poem conveys is the living organism that results.

One problem in our secular societies today is that the traditional connection between religion and poetry, and therefore between the language of both, can mean that those who reject religion also object to a language of ethics they characterize, because of its poeticism, as quasi-religious. That is a serious mistake. We need such language to access the full spectrum of our human ways of knowing, especially moral intuition, imagination, and creativity. There are also effects on the practice of ethics if we restrict the use of poetic language. As moral theologian Ronald Rolheiser says, "When the surface — [the physical] — is all that there is, it's hard to be enchanted by anything, to see the depth that's uncovered by poetry, aesthetics, altruism, religion, faith, and love. And it's especially difficult to understand community. When the physical is all that there is . . . it becomes difficult even just to understand our real connection with each other."[8]

In secular societies we do not use religious language to debate public policy, but we have no robust, comprehensive, and widely shared vocabulary of the imagination — that is, no substitute language — to replace it. But while philosophers, scientists, politicians, and bureaucrats lack such a language, people who create and use popular culture (especially in the genre of science fiction) may be developing their own language of the imagination. Some of us may disagree with the aesthetics of these productions or even the morality of them. The fact is, however, that they *do* explore many universal and existential problems and, often, quite effectively. They're creative. They're imaginative. They're even "poetic." Popular culture, in fact, is the chief venue of secular myths. From an ethics perspective, we need to pay close attention to what those myths are.

Nevertheless, we lack a secular ethical vocabulary to express institutional and societal ethical concerns such as respect for and protection of important values in those contexts. In the past, we used religious language even in non-religious settings such as courts, legislatures, and the public square. Many people, even those who are religious, recognize this is not possible today, if for no other reason than the existence of many different religions in each society. In contrast, we have a well-developed commercial language, and increasingly a bureaucratic language, that is applied far beyond the confines of commerce and bureaucracy. A major problem and danger is that these languages are being used in contexts where they distort the ethical issues raised.[9] For instance, to discuss new reproductive technologies (NRTS), or therapeutic cloning and embryo stem-cell research using only commercial or bureaucratic language means we either lose the ethical dimensions that must be taken into account in considering these technologies, or confuse these ethical dimensions with material and commercial ones.

I was asked recently to review a draft UNESCO report dealing with the funding of ethics research. The report used the term *ethics deliverables* to describe an important criterion in choosing which projects would be funded. But what does using language that is managerial, bureaucratic, and corporate in a field like ethics do to that field? Depending upon what constitutes a "deliverable," and to whom the deliverable is to be delivered, certain kinds of ethics research will not receive grants. Moreover, if "deliverable" means "economically beneficial," and the recipients of these deliverables are businesses, this deforms the field and devalues work that corporations view as less useful to them than other kinds of work. The greatest danger is one I mentioned earlier: that the ethics is designed to "fit" the technology — that is, to not inhibit its development and use — rather than the technology being brought into line with the ethics.

We need to find a new poetic language for ethics that is acceptable to, and can accommodate, everyone. We need such a language to deal not with "deliverables," but with the much larger challenge of finding a shared ethics. I have spoken above of our need for some new concepts — in particular, a concept of the secular sacred. We should keep the requirements for implementing that concept in mind when seeking a poetry of ethics — a language that can give us access to reason, but also take us beyond it in searching for a shared ethics — because that concept's existence, content, and capacity to contribute to better ethical decision-making will largely depend upon the language, especially the metaphors, analogies, and rhetoric, as well as the modes of argumentation we choose to employ in "ethics talk."

The Nature and Function of "Ethics Talk"

Ethicists often speak of *ethics talk*, and I have used that term already in this book. Such talk is not merely interesting conversation, but a methodology for exploring a situation from an ethics perspective — it's a means of ethical analysis. As well, there is a difference between using words to *describe* a situation and the use of words as tools to *do* something — that is, using words as a "verbal act" in that the use of the words changes the facts. In psychiatry, law, and ethics, words function as "verbal acts."[10] A psychiatrist uses words as a therapeutic tool to heal the patient; a judge changes reality in ruling a person guilty or not guilty; and an ethicist working on a real case can have an analogous impact when facilitating an ethics analysis of a situation.

If, as many philosophers and others believe, language is fundamental to being human — fundamental to becoming fully our "self," relating to others, experiencing our world, and finding meaning in life — then we must take great care in using it. That care must extend to needing clear justifications for any restrictions on language and communication (we must respect freedom of speech, freedom of association, and academic freedom) and to protecting people against serious abuse of language and communication (for instance, hate speech and certain kinds of pornography). In short, we must take great care in setting the boundaries, whether positive or negative, on our use of language.

We must also keep in mind that using language to define and label is not a neutral activity and is often an exercise of power. Therefore definition and labelling must be undertaken ethically, especially when the impact is to demonize others or to include or exclude certain people or ideas, as is often the case with definition and labelling. Because language activates our emotions, imagination, and intuition, our choice of words in discussing a given issue can determine our ethical perceptions and judgements about it: one person's "terrorist" can be another's "freedom-fighter."

We bond to each other and form societies by sharing stories we all buy into. The stories encompass our most fundamental and important values, principles, attitudes, beliefs, and myths. The poet Clive Doucet, speaking about the role stories play in forming nations, says:

> Nations are like icebergs. Eighty per cent of them are invisible. The ice below the surface of the ocean creates a platform on which the beautiful white columns of the iceberg are able to thrust toward the sky. But without that undersea platform, the largest part, the iceberg turns over and is no more. Stories are the platform on which a nation floats.[11]

Stories are also the platform on which a global community — and a shared ethics — must float, which means the language and words we use to tell those stories are immensely important. Our challenge is to find the language to tell the stories that will allow us to find a shared ethics. We must see that challenge as an exploration of the human heart, mind, and spirit, an adventure, a struggle to understand, if we are to find the stories we need.

In the end, perhaps the best that we can do in our search for a shared ethical language is to search for consensus through dialogue and through the articulation of (as much as possible) inclusive images and metaphors. And we should see the effort as an ongoing dynamic process, not an endpoint.

Metaphors

I believe the metaphor of a double helix can help us to understand what is involved in making the ethical progress that must accompany our scientific progress, and help us to take into account and balance our various ways of knowing. Imagine these ways of knowing as being like the individual genes that together make up a functioning genome, a genome that results in an organic whole — whether a living single cell, a plant, an insect, an animal, or a human. This metaphor captures how I see them operating collectively. Just as genes code for and interact with one another and the environment to create the elements that make up our physical being, so these ways of knowing code for, and interact with, one another and the environment to create the non-physical realities that are of the essence of being human. Moreover, just as a gene may operate in one way at one time or in one environment, and in another way at another time or in a different environment (a phenomenon called pleiotropy), the same is true of our ways of knowing.

Constant movement and dynamism are involved in all aspects of doing ethics. I have been working with two metaphors to try to represent that constant movement and dynamism: a double helix (like the the DNA double helix) and a constellation of stars.[12] I see the "ethics process" as moving up or, sometimes, down the ethics helix, or moving from star to star in the ethics constellation. Note that the terms *doing ethics* and *ethics talk* also imply an ongoing process like the movement forward and backward along the helix, or the movement from star to star.

Together, the metaphors of the helix and constellation may tell us something else. The DNA helix exists, in fact — it is a factual, functioning entity when it constitutes a gene, and the genes a genome. The constellation, as far as we know, is entirely of our imagination. Yet both images are equally useful metaphors in helping us to discover new insights about what we need in our search for ethics: both inspire wonder and awe, but one depends on its factual integrity and the other on imagination. In short, these images combined suggest that facts, imagination, the integration of these two qualities, and being open to wonder and awe are essential components in "doing ethics."

In debates about ethics, people at the poles are very certain of their arguments and in interacting with one another create a mutual tension that can provide ethical insight — and sometimes an ethical stalemate when both groups refuse to budge. They are often represented in ethics as the two poles of a spectrum — or sometimes as facing points in the arc of a pendulum. But I think the helix is a better model, and the double helix an even better one, because ethics does not move alone and detached from another reality, but in conjunction with that other reality, whether that other reality is scientific research, formulating public policy, or treating sick people. The helix also shows that when we move forward away from one pole and toward another — as we do constantly — we do not then go back to the same place from which we originally started, as we would in a pendulum model. Rather, we go above that place, although we can also travel down the helix, even below the point at which we started. In coming back above the place from which we started, our challenge is to incorporate the ethics insights we have found on the journey with what we still need of the older ethics knowledge in order to bring all of it forward into the present. That the DNA helix repeats at regular intervals allows us to capture this idea in the metaphor.

The metaphor of the helix is valuable also because it goes beyond representing the tension between the poles, although it incorporates that. It's the "going beyond" that is most important. For want of a better word, I describe it as an extra dimension (although I should probably say "dimensions"). What the metaphor of the ethical double helix suggests is that the interaction between science and ethics provides us with building blocks for a shared ethics that would not otherwise be available. Just as the DNA double helix codes for genes, and the genes for proteins, which constitute all living matter, so the metaphorical helix codes for ideas, thoughts, insights, judgements, and all these together code for the conceptual bases (whether intellectual, emotional, spiritual, or religious) through which we find meaning in life and upon which we establish families, institutions, and societies. The discovery of pleiotropy — that, depending on the circumstances, the same gene can produce different proteins — also resonates with the metaphorical helix. Depending on the circumstances, the same ideas, concepts, or principles can play different roles and produce different results.

That one can imagine moving forward and backward along the helix links it, for me, as a metaphor to the ancient wisdom in the Aboriginal saying I mentioned previously — that in making important decisions for society we must look backward seven generations and forward seven generations. The "repetitive renewal" aspect of the helix also reflects the idea that not only our body, but also, some argue, our mind renews itself every seven years.[13] The helix, in circling back on itself at a higher level, also anticipates the idea that some happenings can be cyclical and, at the same time, progress.

It's also important to point out that the helix differs from a pendulum in that it does not represent simply finding a balance between the two poles, as a pendulum would. Sometimes the best ethical response is a balance, but not always. In short, some compromises are ethical and others are not, just as some consensuses are ethical and others are not, and some majority votes are ethical while others are not — democratic decisions are only as ethical as those who vote. Neither a balance of competing claims or values nor majority approval is an automatic ethical justification.

The metaphor of the constellation, too, implies wonder and uncertainty. It shows how through the use of imagination, creativity, and hope, we can derive patterns from points of light in space, which we can then use as guides to give our lives meaning. And both the helix and the constellation imply interconnectedness.

Complexity and Uncertainty

Importantly, both the helix and the constellation imply complexity and uncertainty, which often co-exist. We have much work to do in developing an ethics of complexity. And learning to live comfortably with uncertainty is a fundamental requirement for "doing ethics." We make many ethical mistakes because we are uncomfortable with, or even fearful of, uncertainty, and we often deal with our anxiety by trying to change unavoidable uncertainty to certainty and end up with false certainty. We need to learn to hold certainty and uncertainty in creative tension. So, how should we deal with uncertainty and doubt? And how do experiences of uncertainty, doubt, and the unknown relate to ethics?

The German philosopher Theodor Adorno said, "The highest form of morality is not to feel at home in one's own home."[14] I take that to mean that we must always be questioning our ethics if we are to remain ethical; we must always be uncertain and listen to that uncertainty. I suggest that the experience of ethical uncertainty and doubt is common to all, and is a requirement for acting ethically. As part of a shared base, we could agree on the need to protect the conditions that will allow people to experience ethical uncertainty and doubt. Indeed, perhaps we have to be comfortable with uncertainty and doubt before we can experience wonder and awe at contemplating the unknown. I've thought for a long time that a sense of awe and wonder about what we know we *don't* know is an important element of high "ethical intelligence." It generates humility in the face of our amazing new knowledge and that, in turn, generates respect, perspective, and restraint.

Truth

Once we accept the unavoidable presence of uncertainty, our understanding of truth and consensus in ethics shifts. We no longer speak about truth only in an objective scientific sense, nor do we speak about it only in a metaphysical sense. Rather, the kind of ethical truths we look for, those on which we can agree, are forms of "temporal truth" — always open to challenge, of course, and to change. Some of us would see any such change as a change in the truth; others would see it as a clarification or correction of our previously inadequate or mistaken articulation of truth. In other words, the concept of temporal truth in no way denies that there can be Eternal Truth. Rather, if we believe in Eternal Truth, we hope that what we see as temporal truths are partial manifestations of it.

The way in which I see truth can be described with another metaphor, one that can be added to those of the double helix and constellation. I start by imagining that which we are looking at in order to discover the truth about it — whether it's a person, an object, an idea, a theory, a principle, a belief. I then imagine it in the centre of a big circle, and imagine all the people who are looking at it standing around the circumference of that circle, each holding a light. The lights are of different kinds and have different-coloured lenses, and a few of them fail to work (their batteries are dead) or they show a distorted image (what they show is not true). Some of the lights were invented recently and show us truths we didn't know before; others are old and show us truths that we still need.

The different-coloured and different kinds of lights reveal different aspects of the entity we are looking at. These aspects are not the same, but they are all aspects of its truth. Moreover, just as combining blue and yellow gives green, the combination of two or more lights can show us a new reality, different from those shown by each light separately. When these different aspects are so compatible that they can all be combined, we get the white light of ethical insight. This metaphor captures the idea that there can be equally valid but different versions of the truth about something, rather than one person or body having the full and exclusive truth and others having no access to it. Each version of the truth might or might not be held in common by a large number of people, who might or might not realize that commonality.

Sometimes, however, two different-coloured lights will show us that we have conflicting values and then must make a difficult choice between those values. For instance, a value of caring for individual patients tells us that we should provide all cancer treatments that are likely to be beneficial. A value of protection of the common good tells us we should not do so if that will exhaust health-care resources and bankrupt the system to the detriment of people with other illnesses. Such values conflicts are often found in situations having to do with the protection of public heath. The values of liberty and autonomy of individuals to "decide for themselves what may be done to them" are pre-empted by compulsory treatment and quarantine when the illnesses from which those individuals suffer pose a serious health threat to the community.

Some of the most difficult conflicts to deal with ethically arise when the values that should govern at one level of doing ethics conflict with those at another level. There are four levels: micro or individual; meso or institutional; macro or societal; and mega or global. For example, at the individual ethical level, a physician has "a primary obligation of personal care" to each patient — the "best interests" of the patient being treated must take priority. At the meso or hospital level, a hospital needs to keep within its budget and ethically must use its resources efficiently, with the interests of all patients in mind. This can mean that a certain treatment will not be available to an individual patient who could benefit from it. In such circumstances, the physician must act as a reasonable physician would and try to obtain the treatment for the patient, but if she is unsuccessful, that is not a breach of ethics on her part. In my view, however, failing to tell the patient that there is a potentially beneficial treatment they will not be given, which gives the patient an opportunity to seek it elsewhere, would be a breach of ethics by the physician. Many physicians adamantly reject the idea that they have any such obligation.

The idea of seeing the multifaceted truth of something through the use of different-coloured lights is analogous to the idea that we can see different aspects of reality through the various ways of human knowing — or, for example, through the lenses of different disciplines such as philosophy, psychology, religion, science, and the social sciences, or through methodologies such as establishing the cultural universality of some institutions, beliefs, values, perceptions, or ideas. We can consider these various ways of exploring to be different "lights" that together have the capacity to show multiple aspects of a reality.

My justification for adopting the basic presumption that there exists an extrinsic reality we can perceive in various ways — that reality is a truth — rather than taking the view that reality is a culturally constructed mirage, as some would argue, is that the former stance is preferable on many counts. My presumption is closer to traditional approaches; it puts the burden of proof that change is justified on those challenging the status quo, which is as it should be; and it's more protective of persons, society, values, symbols, and institutions. So my

justification for assuming that what we perceive as a reality truly exists is pragmatic in the sense that I choose it
because it's the most useful approach, but my premise is
also that any given reality has an essential nature — it has
principled content, and there is a truth about it.

The idea of a "multi-part truth" leads me to another
point: I believe that the idea that nothing is true unless we
can scientifically prove it is getting in the way of finding a
shared ethics. Rather, we should see science as just one
lens on the truth. And what we see as the truth, even scientific truth, can change over time. We need to
differentiate between when such change occurs in our
perceptions of a reality, and when the change occurs in the
reality itself. Why couldn't we say that for medieval people it was true the world was flat because what they could
perceive of it was flat? For us, it's true that the world is a
sphere because we can now perceive it that way, but that
is not inconsistent with our day-to-day experience of it as
flat. But might we see it as something else in the future
(some part of a larger whole, for example)? Or all or none
of these, depending on the lens through which we view
the world? Take the example of light — seen as a wave it
has one set of characteristics, seen as particles another set.
But both are equally "true" descriptions of light — or, at
least, they both allow us to explain aspects of the behaviour of light. In short, it may be our perceptions that
change, rather than the nature of what we perceive.
Applied to moral principles, such an understanding
allows us to postulate the existence of a stable moral base
that exists and that we can all share, while at the same

time acknowledging that what we can share is a reflection of what we can see and find of it at any given time.

Language as Declarative, Not Constitutive, of Ethics

Earlier in this chapter, I discussed the importance of our choice of language in "doing ethics." It is also important for us to decide upon the function of language both in establishing ethics and in finding a shared ethics. In my view, through language we articulate the ethics that can constitute a shared base that pre-exists its expression. In other words, we don't create ethics through the language we use; rather, ethics already exists in some external source, whether God or natural morality, or as an intrinsic part of human nature, and language is the tool we use to articulate it. Whatever the source of ethics, we humans are by our nature ethics-seeking creatures; language, stories, and myths are the tools we use to identify and articulate the ethics we find. In the same way, human rights pre-exist their enactment in declarations, charters, and constitutions — those instruments are but one way, although an important one, of articulating them.

Earlier, I described a concept of *human ethics* I proposed should be adopted as a companion concept to that of human rights and its often unarticulated companion concept, that of human responsibilities. It is easy to envision human ethics as intrinsic to being human, as pre-existing some formal or official implementation in concrete situations. Human ethics is, we can say, closer to the natural, and less legalistic, than human rights is often seen as being — although I hasten to add that I see human rights as an important aspect of natural law. Natural law adherents believe in an unwritten body of universal moral principles that underlie the legal norms we enact in positive law — that is, the written rules and regulations enacted by government — and believe that the latter should conform to the deeper moral principles.

But if all humans truly have an innate ethical sense, how can we account for so much diversity in the way we talk about morality? We need to recognize that while there can be many differences in the way we talk about morality, the content of our morality can be the same. As I've explained previously, I believe that in the West we make a serious mistake when we so often start our discussions of ethics and morality from a point of disagreement. This overemphasizes our disagreements and causes us hardly to notice that there is much we can agree on, whatever the basis for the beliefs, principles, or values on which we agree.

The theologian-philosopher Bernard Lonergan describes the process of going from experience to insight to judgement as being the process of how we know, and know that we know — and as being innately human.[15] I see no reason why this is any less true of ethical knowing than of scientific knowing or mathematical knowing, or any other kind of knowing. If that process is a universal one (common to all humans everywhere and across time), we could propose that it could be the basis of a "universal vision," to use Lonergan's term. Our task, then, is to find the shared content of that vision. The fact that judgement is involved in the process means that we will disagree in certain situations. It also means we must be able to live comfortably with uncertainty, because the need for judgement in a situation often means that it is one of uncertainty.

Might Jürgen Habermas's insight that language and communication are innate to being human, and therefore a foundation for a shared ethics,[16] be yet another way to express the possibility of the universal vision that Lonergan describes? The same questions present themselves in philosopher Søren Kierkegaard's concept that morality is linked to protecting in each person the power to become fully themselves.[17] Kierkegaard argues that we must safeguard each person's power to become fully themselves if each of us is to have the means to develop our own authentic identity, which includes a sense of morality and ethics. When we respect and protect that power, we are acting morally, and when we do not, we are acting immorally. Might all these philosophers be expressing in different ways a universal idea about human morality and ethics: that there is a universal core we must struggle to identify in ourselves as both individuals and societies, and that there are also other features that vary from culture to culture, era to era, religion to religion? That approach accommodates both a shared core consisting of some central features — a shared ethical base and, depending on the issue and circumstances, to greater or lesser extents a shared ethics — and the variability of other features.

Habermas also proposes that morality takes the form of different language games in different contexts. I believe that while this may be true on the surface, ultimately we are engaged in a single unifying morality "game." More-over, I believe that although language is an important form of the game, it's not, as Habermas argues, the only or ultimate form. That would be making language God. It's interesting to contemplate Habermas's theory along-side the opening words of John's Gospel: "In the beginning was the Word, and the Word was with God, and the Word was God."[18] The Greek *logos*, however, does not refer to "word" in the linguistic sense; it refers to the mind — in this case the mind of God. Likewise, whatever its ultimate source, ethics emanates most immediately from the human mind.

Habermas's concept is nevertheless important in at least two respects. First, it guides us to a crucial insight about the central task of ethicists: to address the question of whether there are certain overlapping rules that are common to all language games of moral life. To a large extent that's what I'm trying to do, but as I've explained, I believe that moral life is based on more than just lan-guage games. Language games, technical ones at least, are largely the territory, the province, and the function of academics, scholars, and intellectuals, especially philoso-phers. The search for a shared ethics that I'm envisioning has to include everyone if it is to function as I hope it might. It must also conform to people's lived experience — how we, in general, experience being human. In that regard, it is important to state that I do not see poetry as a language game. Rather, it reflects, creates, and communi-cates elements of the human spirit that are integral to finding our individual and shared human identity. And

finding that shared identity is closely bound up with finding a shared ethics.

The concept of a language game is also useful because
once we are aware of the rules of the game, we can begin
to see how the metaphors we use give shape to the game
and change its structure. Consequently, becoming aware
of these linguistic structures is crucial in "doing ethics."
For example, we need to identify exclusionary negative
metaphors (for instance, those that result in stigmatization, scapegoating, and discrimination) that lead to
unethical conduct and replace them with more constructive language, symbols, and metaphors that build
compassion and inclusion — that is, ethical conduct.[19] I
hasten to add that in saying that I am not endorsing political correctness, as such, and its devastating impact on
freedom of speech and academic freedom. Rather, I am
arguing that the ethicist is like a poet[20]: he or she must not
only search out old metaphors and eliminate those that
are harmful to others, but also string together new ones
that broaden our moral base and ensure that certain fundamental rules are being obeyed.[21] In short, through
language the ethicist has power and control over "doing
ethics."

Of course, the words *power and control* should cause
our ethics neurons to fire. They bring to mind the concept
of political correctness and how it can be used as a form
of control. Is the ethicist's high degree of control over setting the ethics agenda, much like peoples' use of political
correctness in some instances, antithetical to fostering the
freedom necessary for each person to become them-

selves? Is the ethicist's control anti-ethical? The answer, as it is to so many ethical questions, is that it depends. But let me address that question with another one: might it be that the utilitarians and the principle-based ethicists are seeking the same freedom for each person, but through different lenses, approaches, philosophies, or values? In that case, where the ethicists disagree is on how best to ensure that each person can realize the freedom to become herself or himself, not on the central importance of the freedom to each person. If so, they have more in common than they believe, and this could not only dispel fear about the ethicists' control of language, it might be an important insight in helping us to find a shared ethics.

I believe that part of our freedom is that we must be free to make mistakes (and, one hopes, learn from them) in the process of becoming fully ourselves. I believe that we each must find ethics, morality, and spirituality for ourselves if we are to experience them authentically, as intrinsic to ourselves and not something imposed on us from outside. That is not to say that we don't need outside assistance — we certainly do. And it might be that we especially need such help when we are children and young people; as adults, we need to move on and rediscover or redefine ethics, morality, and spirituality for ourselves if we are to experience full development of these capacities.

In this chapter, I have been speaking of ethics and ethicists, poets and poetry, language and ethics. Many years ago, a very dear friend, Dr. Norbert Gilmore, told me something I've never forgotten: "It takes only one generation to turn a poet's words into bullets." That became a kind of mantra for me. The most important challenge for all of us, but especially for ethicists, poets, and philosophers, is that of how to turn bullets — or bombs or bio-weapons — into poets' words.

III

OLD NATURE,
NEW SCIENCE:

RESPECTING NATURE,
THE NATURAL, AND LIFE

WE HAVE BEEN talking about finding agreement on the substantive content of a shared ethics. Now I want to look at whether we can agree on how we should go about looking for that content — the process or procedures we might use to try to find that shared ethics. In particular, as we look at respect for life in the context of the new technoscience, can we agree on a starting point for our ethical analysis? That is, can we share a basic presumption on which to found it? Presumptions are process principles, but they, too, are far from neutral in affecting the outcomes of our decisions. The law has an old saying that sums up this reality: form is no mere formality.

Just as people have challenged my concept of the secular sacred in the past, they have challenged both the concept of the natural and my proposal that we should adopt a primary presumption in favour of it as a starting point for ethical analysis. So let me explain what I mean by a presumption in favour of the natural — in particular, in relation to human nature — and why I think it is a crucial, fundamental concept, both in searching for a shared ethics and in "doing ethics."

The views and arguments I set out in this chapter in defence of the natural and its importance are diametrically opposed to an increasingly prevalent, postmodern, politically correct approach that neutralizes language to abolish difference. For instance, a general article in the McGill Centre for Research and Teaching on Women (MCRTW) *Bulletin* on "Philosophy, Sex, Gender" claims that natural differences between the sexes and in gender don't exist — they are just constructs. I disagree strongly, but defining the natural is not easy. That difficulty does not mean, however, that it does not exist or is an unimportant concept. Moreover, we might even disagree in some instances as to what is or is not natural. In particular, it is extremely difficult to define the natural in a way that is not either under- or over-inclusive.

Exploring the Natural

Before proceeding, and at the risk of overgeneralization, there are three broad concepts of the natural I want to identify and differentiate: one that it is purely biological; one that it is purely a cultural construct; and one that involves a combination of biology and culture. I take the last view: that the biological is an essential substrate of the natural, including human nature, and in some instances the natural might be no more than the biological. But the natural, again including human nature, also encompasses the realities, some of them physical ones, that emerge from the interaction of biology and culture — as new epigenetic research is now showing us. Consequently, I strongly disagree with those who claim there is no such entity as the natural or human nature and that what we see as such is simply a social construction that changes over time, either by chance or choice.[1]

The dangers of rejecting a concept of the natural — for example, of human nature — include this: if there is no essential human nature, then no technologizing of that nature is dehumanizing. In other words, such a rejection serves to legitimate the technological project, because then humans do not have a nature that must be safeguarded, but a history that can be rewritten for the future through technological interventions.[2] It is a powerful endorsement of the technological imperative: have technology; must use. Another danger of rejecting a concept of the natural is that we lose the distinction between using technology "to repair nature when it fails" and using it to realize what would be an impossible outcome through natural processes, a distinction that can help us to differentiate between ethical and unethical uses of technology. Repairing nature is, as a rule, less ethically troublesome than is doing the naturally impossible.

We have no option, however, but to choose between an ethics primarily grounded in nature or primarily grounded in technology. This is a critically important choice when we consider the ethics of interventions on human nature made possible by the new technologies. That is, we must choose the basic presumption on which we will base our ethical analysis, and through which we will decide what we must, may, or should not do with that technoscience.

I may seem to overemphasize the biological component of the natural, especially of human nature, and to underemphasize its cultural component. That is because our new scientific powers to alter the former are unprecedented, and this book focuses on the technoscience through which those powers are exercised. I want to stress, however, that we are also facing a corresponding growth in our power to alter the cultural component of the natural, in the form of unprecedented information and communications technologies.

It's also worth noting that at the same time as we have had such a strong focus on the biological components of the natural because of new technoscience, we have had an equally strong focus on its cultural components. Identity-based social movements such as feminism, and groups fighting for equal rights for disabled people and for gay people, emphasize the latter. Doing so is part of their strategy to achieve social change. We might not be able to change our biology (at least in the past), but we can change our culturally constructed attitudes to that biology, and in turn that can transform what we see as natural and, therefore, as requiring respect.

Oxford University biologist Richard Dawkins calls units of deep cultural information passed on from generation to generation *memes*.[3] Genes and memes are companion concepts: genes are the biological DNA we pass on to our descendants; memes are the deep cultural concepts that we, likewise, pass on. Dawkins argues that in both cases a "survival of the fittest" principle applies — members of a species with genes or memes best adapted to survival in their environment will prevail over those who are least adapted. To be clear, however, my emphasis on the biological is not meant to diminish or detract from the importance of culture in establishing, maintaining, and sometimes changing the natural.

Paradoxically, the two diametrically opposed views — that human nature is only biology or that it is only culture — are being strongly promoted today to the detriment of a balanced view. The intense rationalists promote the "pure biological" view; they espouse the "genes R us" or "gene machine" idea — that we are nothing more than the product of our genes.[4] Meanwhile, those who believe that human nature is simply a social construct promote the "pure culture" view; they believe that human nature is infinitely malleable.[5] Indeed, the adherents of this latter idea often reject any biological givens, such as essential differences between men and women. They argue that even such differences are culturally constructed.[6] Again, I reject both of these approaches. My position is that some elements that constitute the natural in human nature are intrinsic to it and, therefore, non-negotiable. Even if we have the power to change them, we should not do so. They should be regarded as secular sacred. Some of these elements are biological, and some are a combination of biology and culture. It is their totality that makes up the natural in human nature. I will explore these elements more fully in our discussion of transhumanism.

The view that human nature is simply a social construction might seem an unlikely one in our intensely genetics-focused age, but often it comes cloaked in forms other than a direct proposition. Arguments that men and women are just the same, or that it makes no difference to the "best interests" of a child whether a child has a parent of each sex or two parents of the same sex ("genderless parenting"), are based on such a view. I hasten to point out here that the acceptance of innate differences and their importance is not to endorse or accept inequality and wrongful discrimination. And it's true that natural differences — for instance, between men and women — and ideas of the unnatural — for instance, in relation to homosexuality — have been the basis for horrible breaches of human ethics and human rights. But that does not mean that the only acceptable way to respond to differences is either to deny that they exist or to say they are of no importance, two strategies that have been used extensively over the last twenty years. Rather, we should recognize and respond ethically to such differences. In short, we can both recognize difference and respect equality, and those who claim that is impossible and a contradiction in terms are, in my view, wrong. I also want to make it clear that I am not endorsing a "separate but equal" doctrine in its classical sense. Rather, the ethical treatment of differences depends on which differences are being recognized and why and how they are dealt with.

Let's look at same-sex marriage. Its advocates reject a two-institution — marriage and civil unions — approach to the recognition of committed adult relationships. They argue that separate cannot be equal — that the mere fact of separation itself constitutes inequality. But there is a difference between separate but equal and different but equal. Separate but equal means that two entities are inherently the same but are treated as separate. That is discrimination. Different but equal means that two entities are not the same, that the difference between them justifies treating them separately, but they are treated equally. That is the antithesis of discrimination. The same but separate and equal is second-class citizenship or worse. Different but equal is not.

To summarize my position in advance of the argument, in one sentence: one can be, as I am, against same-sex marriage *and* against discrimination against homosexual people.[7]

At its broadest, the highly sensitive and contentious question we must answer in the same-sex marriage debate is: What should be the norm (to which there will always need to be exceptions) on which families are established in our society? Do we want to keep the biological links between parents and children — that is, a natural biological reality — as that norm? Or should the norm be two adults' committed relationship to each other — that is, the concepts of marriage and family are merely social constructs? Opposite-sex marriage establishes the former; including same-sex marriage in marriage, the latter. Asked another way, should we replace natural parenthood with legal parenthood as the basic norm, as same-sex marriage does? If we decide that we want marriage to continue to uphold natural parenthood as the norm, then ethically we must provide for exceptions to that norm. That means we will as a society have responsibilities to support and protect same-sex families — although, in my view, we should not actively help to create them.

At the heart of the disagreement between people who support same-sex marriage and those who oppose it is whether the fact that opposite-sex couples represent a naturally, inherently procreative relationship, and same-sex couples do not, constitutes a difference that justifies separate but equal institutions — marriage and civil unions — to publicly recognize committed, adult pair-bonding. If, as same-sex marriage advocates claim, a two-institutions approach is discriminatory in its essence, it is unacceptable. To decide whether that is the case requires looking at, first, the context in which separate but equal institutions are proposed; second, whether there is a relevant difference between the institutions; and third, the reasons for adopting the two-institutions approach.

Marriage is a compound right: the right to marry and found a family. Opposite-sex marriage establishes as the norm and institutionalizes the inherently procreative relationship between a man and a woman, and in doing so establishes children's rights with respect to links to their biological parents and families. Because same-sex marriage is not an inherently procreative relationship, recognizing it necessarily negates that norm, and with that, children's rights in this regard. If we want marriage to continue to establish and protect those rights of children in general, marriage cannot be extended to include same-sex couples. (Unlike same-sex couples, infertile opposite-sex married couples, or ones who don't want children, do not transgress the general norm.) Yet same-sex couples deserve equal protection in their relationships. This can be provided by legally recognizing civil unions — which do not implicate children's rights — as France and the United Kingdom have recently done.

This is a "separate but equal" approach, which is often rejected as discrimination. But we accept such an approach in some cases. For instance, we accept that separate schools for girls and boys — that is, separation on the basis of sex, but not on the basis of race — can be equal, and this is not seen as discriminatory by most people. In other words, sometimes separate but equal is ethically acceptable. The central issue is: What is required in terms of respect? Some reasons for undertaking an act manifest respect, but undertaking the same act for other reasons can mean showing disrespect. In short, the *same* act can be discrimination or not, *depending on the reasons for undertaking it.* To reject same-sex marriage in order to affirm, in the public square, moral or other objections to homosexual people is a failure of respect and is discrimination. To reject it because marriage could no longer embody the inherently procreative relationship between a man and a woman, and thereby establish children's rights with respect to their biological parents and wider biological family, is not discrimination.

Complementarity in parenting — a child's need for both a male parent and a female parent — is an issue raised by same-sex marriage. We are rapidly increasing our knowledge about the interaction of the biological and the cultural, including in human nature, through research in epigenetics. Epigenetics is the study of the interaction of genes and the environment, and how each affects and modifies the other in an ongoing process. For instance, baby rats have a gene that codes for nurturing behaviour. It needs to be activated (imprinted) by their mothers licking them during a short, critical window of time soon after their birth. If they are not licked in that period, the gene shuts down permanently and, as adults, they will not nurture their own offspring (as is true of rats without the gene, even if they have been nurtured).[8] Scientists have recently launched a project to map the human epigenome. The human genome — all the genes that make up a human — has already been mapped, and now scientists want to identify the genes that depend for their expression on interaction with the environment.

It can be difficult to draw the line as to where the natural ends, when culture is deliberately used to modify biology. For example, it seems that humans have an innate repugnance to killing other humans. It is possible that repugnance could be genetically based — we don't know whether it is or isn't. But we do know that soldiers who will be engaged in close hand-to-hand combat can be psychologically deprogrammed in a way that enables them to kill other humans at close range. Their resulting capacity to do that would not be natural; but the same capacity in soldiers who have faced certain vicissitudes might be considered natural. Likewise, being born an identical twin is a natural occurrence when it happens by chance, but is a non-natural one when it is the result of a deliberate intervention. These examples provide clues as to the distinction between the natural and the non-natural: what is or is not natural is not simply a matter of an end result, but involves how that end result came about — in particular, whether there was human intervention that gave rise to it, and whether the intent of that intervention was to achieve a particular result.

The natural and the non-natural are sometimes deliberately confused, usually to argue that changing the natural through the use of new technoscience does not raise any special or novel ethical issues, by making a non-natural intervention analogous to a natural occurrence. The case of identical twins is one example; identical twins occur naturally, the argument goes, so why is it unacceptable to create them artificially by splitting an embryo at an early stage of its development? Another argument of the same kind says that choosing certain characteristics of our children through new reproductive and genetic technologies is no different from choosing our sexual partners for procreation. This approach looks only at outcomes, not at means and intentions. What is natural, however, does not depend only on outcomes, but also on the means used to realize those outcomes. So, for example, genetically modified food is not natural, which means we must show that creating and producing that kind of food is justified in any given circumstances. In general, when we are in doubt about whether an intervention or its outcome falls within the definition of the natural, we should apply a precautionary principle: we should assume that they do not do so until the contrary is shown, and therefore undertaking that intervention and its outcome must both be justified. In other words, to repeat, we should work from a basic presumption in favour of the natural.

Some people who reject religion will reject my basic presumption in favour of the natural as being religious or quasi-religious. But even if that were true, which we can argue about, that does not mean the presumption should be rejected. There is no way to avoid making a choice of basic presumption. We must all do so, and where we disagree is in whether or not one in favour of the natural is preferable. In the past when our powers to change the natural were extremely limited, we allowed intervention until it was shown to be harmful. I believe that the new powers science and technology have given us make this no longer an acceptable approach.

I want to make it clear that I am not opposed to altering the natural — in either its biological or its cultural components. Rather, I argue that we should have a *presumption* in favour of respecting the natural, which means that unless we can show that we are justified in intervening on or altering it, we should refrain from doing so. That presumption implements a principle of respect for the natural that allows interventions on or changes to the natural that can be justified ethically. Consider an intervention to change a person's genes. To undertake such an intervention to treat a horrible disease might, in some circumstances, be justified. To do so to enhance intelligence when no mental disorder is present would, in my view, never be justified. Likewise, in altering our cultural reality — such as redefining marriage — we must show that we are justified.

A Basic Presumption in Favour of the Natural

The importance of basic presumptions lies in the fact that the person relying on a basic presumption does not have to prove their case; rather, the burden of proof of justification lies with the person claiming that there should be an exception. Consequently, in situations of equal doubt, the position of the person who is favoured by the basic presumption prevails. This difference in burden of proof can be extremely important in determining what we may do, and what we must not do if serious, or possibly serious but unknown or unknowable, risk is present.

Principle-based ethicists believe that some things are inherently wrong and therefore must not be undertaken, no matter how much good could result. The use of a basic presumption in favour of the natural can help such ethicists to establish the outcomes they argue for. For example. scientists found that altering a certain gene in fish resulted in the fish becoming hyper-aggressive to other fish. Later, the scientists found that humans have the same gene. When this research was reported, some journalists called me to ask about the ethics of making the same change to the gene in humans in order to create fearless soldiers. My intuitive reaction was that this would be profoundly unethical — that is, inherently wrong. We can also arrive at the same result by arguing that we must work from a basic presumption in favour of the natural: we would conclude that such a manipulation of the natural can never be justified. This reasoning is an example of using a presumption in favour of the natural as a backup mechanism to validate a conclusion that a certain intervention is inherently wrong — a presumption in favour of the natural supports a principle-based ethics. But even if we reject principle-based ethics in favour of utilitarianism and moral relativism, the presumption gives us a mechanism to conclude that such alterations are unethical. It does so by making us aware that the natural is a "good," and harm to it should be taken into account; that more harm than good can result from certain interventions on the natural; and that those wanting to intervene have the burden of proving that benefits outweigh risks and harms before intervention can be justified.

Another example is in relation to our treatment of animals — an ethical issue of the utmost importance, although it is only noted in passing in this book. Our basic presumption in favour of the natural means that we must show respect for animals in all our interventions that affect them. It means, in particular, that we must be able to justify the way they are treated and the sacrifice of their lives to use them as food. Unless eating meat has a purpose beyond personal self-gratification, it is very difficult to find a justification for taking animal life. British philosopher Roger Scruton argues that offering meat is "the primordial gift to the stranger . . . [and it is not justified] to kill again and again for the sake of a solitary pleasure that neither creates nor sustains any moral ties."[9] Acceptance of this idea would not require us to be vegetarians, but it would require us to justify our treatment of animals used for food and killing them, and that in turn would limit our consumption of meat. In any case, we must never deliberately inflict pain on animals without the most powerful justification, one that is certainly never present in the factory farming of animals used for food, which, even at its best, often involves horrific treatment of animals and is ethically reprehensible.[10]

A basic presumption in favour of the natural avoids the problem of needing to distinguish between good and bad in the natural, except in individual concrete cases, while maintaining general respect for the natural. This is an important protection, given the unprecedented potential for changing nature and the natural opened up by advances in technoscience. Where intervening to change the natural can be shown to be justified, it will be (within limits) ethically acceptable — for example, where the good we will do in helping desperately poor people who lack clean water or food, or those with serious illnesses, far outweighs any risks or harms. The limits are important because certain means are not ethical, no matter how much good is sought in using them. So, for instance, deleting genes for "bad" human characteristics — extreme aggression, anger, jealousy — would never be justified in my view.

Rediscovering Respect for the Natural

I think we have made a mistake in disconnecting ourselves from nature and the natural. Poet and observer of nature Karel Sloane puts it this way: "Humans see themselves, by and large, as separated from the natural world. This separation has also been stratified, placing nature in an inferior position and humans in a superior one."[11] As a result, we have lost a sense of the natural and lost awareness of the need to justify our interventions on it. One way to regain our respect might be to conceptualize nature and the natural as a "public good." That would require both that it be protected and that everyone have access to it.

Nature and the natural have much to teach us that it is difficult and perhaps impossible to learn elsewhere. Sloane's description of nature and her reaction to it provide clues as to what it can teach us: "Nature has no borders. It is everywhere, a living breathing boundaryless observatory. Patterns reveal that nature is orderly while random flux reveals the opposite. This paradox, much to the dismay of my desire for holdfasts, teaches me there is room for both order and chaos."[12] The natural has order, purpose, and meaning, and humans have long used contact with it to find order, purpose, and meaning in their individual and communal lives. But it is also in a state of constant change, including through human intervention. Chaos and uncertainty can result. Experiencing this aspect of nature can help us to learn to live more comfortably with uncertainty in our own lives.

We need order, purpose, and meaning if we are to fully live fully human lives. Without them we face ennui, loss of hope, feelings of disintegration, and meaninglessness — in short, despair and nihilism. Contact with the natural allows us to appreciate that as humans we are part of a much larger order of being, which can be an anti-dote to such responses. And wonderfully, rather than diminishing that appreciation, technoscience augments it by opening up astonishing new realities about our place in the universe. Nature and the natural deserve respect from an anthropocentric perspective. Harm to them can harm important aspects of human life, and this is one, but only one, reason that human interventions on the natural require justification. But having pointed out nature's benefits to humans, I want to emphasize that nature and the natural deserve respect in their own right, not just because they are of benefit to us.

Respect for nature and the natural require close and frequent contact with nature and the natural. The situations that present dangers of loss of contact with nature and the natural may not be immediately obvious; they often come cloaked in the language of progress and promoted as "must-have," luxury, consumer products. Loss of contact with nature is particularly tragic in the case of children. We have no idea what the long-term effects of this will be on individuals, communities and society.

One teacher of eleven-year-old children tells how a student wrote in her class journal that she had never climbed a tree. She longed to do that and watch the sun set. The teacher discovered that many in the class had never climbed a tree, never walked in a field. They had no sense of connection with the natural world or of its fragility or preciousness. Indeed, they were fearful of nature.[13] I have deep concern that many children lack a connection with nature that engenders the respect for the natural required to protect some of our most important shared values. The consequences for our thinking as a society about technoscience, especially the ethics of its uses, could be devastating. Our response, however, should not be to wring our hands in despair. Young people long to experience the wonder and awe of nature and we can help them to do so. To do this is not only a moral undertaking — it is a moral necessity.

I wonder if our loss of contact with nature, especially with animals, has caused us to lose contact with non-rational knowledge — ways of knowing other than reason. So often, only those with whom we can communicate verbally are important and valued. Yet we have much to learn through exchange with the natural world, especially through an appreciation of the complexity of animals' lives and behaviour, and of their modes of communication and social networks.

Psychologists have shown that we jump away from a snake on the path before we have consciously realized the snake is there.[14] Could this be an indication that we have inherited genetic knowledge about nature? Connecting with the natural in itself is a way of knowing — perhaps even one that is genetically based and inherited from generation to generation. It might also be that physicians who are trained to rely mainly on technology to the exclusion of their innate skills in making diagnoses either do not fully develop, or lose, their intuitive, clinical diagnostic skills. And local fishermen observing their environment have often proved to be more accurate in assessing the long-term impact of overfishing on fish stocks than scientists with technical tools, data, and expertise. As these examples demonstrate, we will lose our nature-reading skills if we fail to exercise them.

Rebecca Solnit's book, *A Field Guide to Getting Lost*, was recently reviewed in the *Village Voice*. The reviewer wrote: "We live in an increasingly standardized environment, bouncing from one branch of Starbucks to another, and it's almost impossible to get truly lost thanks to technology. Solnit believes that our fear of not knowing where we are is partly due to our inability to read the language of nature."[15] Her insight links our disconnection from nature to the creation of uncertainty (and, we can add, that disconnection is also linked to our inability to tolerate uncertainty) and the fear that is generated as a result. Ironically, we try to reduce that fear by taking control with technology, which further alienates us from nature. Fortunately, the converse is also true: that being connected with nature can teach us to live more comfortably with uncertainty. "There's an art to attending to the weather, to the route you take, to the landmarks along the way. . . . And there's another art of being at home in the unknown, so that being in its midst isn't cause for panic or suffering."[16]

One future scenario of our loss of contact with nature, or repudiation of it, is that presented by the transhumanists. They believe humans — and human experience, as we know and treasure it — should and will become obsolete, and are working toward that goal. Another scenario — for me a more hopeful one — is that we will recognize what we have lost before it is too late to recapture it, and will once again respect the natural and revere nature. I also hope we will recognize that we are unique in that we have two roles with respect to nature: we are both an integral part of it and, because we alone have the power to destroy it, we must be its protector. With great power comes great responsibility, and nowhere is that more true than in balancing new science and old nature.

In short, a basic presumption in favour of the natural is a principle of fundamental ethical importance. The use of this presumption is justified not only because of its usefulness to a particular culture or group of people — which means that utilitarians would accept it — but, more importantly, because nature in itself is an inherent good. Consequently, a presumption in favour of the natural should be supported by all humans, despite our cultural differences. For the most part, this principle will not need to be imposed. A profound respect and awe for the natural is already interwoven into most of the cultures and religions that give shape to humanity. In fact, the current challenge to our presumption in favour of the natural and respect for nature and the natural is posed by a relatively small group of secular fundamentalists, who hold what I call a "pure-science" worldview. They deal with the ethical dilemmas posed by the technological advances, which are significant and unprecedented, from the starting point of the benefits advances in techno-science might bring and the rights of individuals to decide for themselves how to use these advances. In stark contrast, I believe that when we confront these dilemmas we need to start from a presumption in favour of the natural in order to find the shared ethics that should govern them.

The justification for choosing a presumption in favour of respect for the natural to guide ethical decision-making is that it maintains respect for all living beings and the planet, and the integrity of both; it protects traditional values and wisdom; it places the burden of proof of justification on those intervening to change the natural; and it carries the least downside risk. In this, it embodies and applies the precautionary principle to risk-taking — that is, those who create risks and harms must justify doing so before imposing them, whether those risks are physical or moral ones.

Finally, I want to conclude this general discussion of respect for nature and the natural on a personal note, with a brief story. As a child, my father was an altar boy in a Roman Catholic church in a very small town in the vast Outback of Australia. When I was a small child, he was first an atheist and, later, an agnostic. Later still, I am not sure what his beliefs were. In short, he certainly did not buy into traditional religion, yet he had an enormous respect for nature and the natural that permeated and informed every aspect of his life.

When he was dying, I asked him if he would like to see a priest. He answered wryly, "No, keep those black crows away from me," and questioned why I thought that he would want this. I replied that he was one of the most religious people that I had ever met — although *spiritual* would have been a better word. He laughed and said that was not correct. I explained to him that I found his profound connection with nature, his way of seeing the world, his love of ideas and the "things of the human spirit," an expression of intense spirituality. He smiled and said, "Margo, that is not religion, that's living with the universe." A priest friend to whom I told this story remarked that this was perhaps one of the best definitions of true religion he had ever encountered. The word *religion*, after all, comes from "re ligere" — to bind together — and the universe is the grandest scale on which we can do this.

Thinking about my father's philosophy of life causes me to wonder about the ways in which we might bond constructively and strongly to one another. Does one-on-one bonding eventually self-destruct because, by itself, it can't carry the weight of the relationship? Do we need to buy into something beyond ourselves to find ourselves and others? If so, how do we find this in a secular society and technoscience age? What forces beyond ourselves might we all recognize?

I believe that the most obvious of those forces is nature. Indeed, I believe respect for nature might be the source of respect we have for forces beyond nature — for instance, those made available through new technoscience.

Respect for Life

I now want to explore the relation between respect for the natural and respect for life, in particular human life. I talked earlier about how I believe two principles could found a shared ethics: first, deep respect for all life, in particular human life; and second, profound respect for the human spirit — that is, the metaphysical reality we need to experience in order to live fully human lives and find meaning in life. I've come to believe that respect for nature and the natural underlies both of these principles and, consequently, that using a presumption in favour of the natural as a base for making ethical decisions is of the utmost importance in implementing them in practice. In other words, a presumption in favour of the natural is a way of implementing respect for life and for the human spirit. But it is also a way of implementing respect for nature and the natural because it requires us to know what that respect entails and helps us to work out what we should not do, what we may do, and what we must do, if we are to be ethical.

To determine what respect for nature, especially human nature, and the natural requires, it is helpful to look at the substance of nature, and of human nature, and the respect required by both. Let's start by briefly considering the concept of human dignity — what it means, and what role it does (and should) play in ensuring respect for human life. We also need to look at what respect for human life requires given the possibilities opened up by new reproductive technologies. What we decide is or is not ethical in that context will necessarily affect respect for human life itself, and for future individual human lives. It will also, importantly, affect the nature of the respect we have for the human spirit: some of our most important individual and societal values are intimately connected to reproduction and birth.

Human Dignity

Those who espouse the view that reproductive rights and freedom require that there should be no limits on abortion, or that there should be unfettered access to new reproductive technologies such as cloning, or that euthanasia and assisted suicide should be legalized, view the concept of respect for life as, at best, controversial. Respect for life is seen as interfering with or negating individual rights and freedoms. In this view, respect for life is subordinated to the concept of human dignity, although the goal behind that strategy — to restrict the application of the value of respect for life — is rarely articulated.

A major example of this can be seen in some of the declarations drafted by UNESCO — for instance, those on genetics and the ethics that should govern interventions on the human genome. On many occasions I have tried, to no avail, to have the principle of "respect for all life, in particular human life" included in such documents. There has, however, been a small but ambiguous move toward my position in the final version of the *Universal Declaration on Bioethics and Human Rights*. It now states that "The aims of this Declaration are: . . . to promote respect for human dignity and protect human rights, by ensuring respect for the life of human beings, and fundamental freedoms, consistent with international human rights law." It is important to note that respect for human life is made subordinate to promoting human dignity and human rights, both of which are principles used to argue, for example, for the legalization of euthanasia and physician-assisted suicide. Moreover, the way in which the respect for life provision in the *Universal Declaration on Bioethics and Human Rights* is drafted, "respect for the life of human beings" would exclude any right to life for a fetus, even a viable one, in countries such as Canada, where fetuses do not fall within the legal definition of "human being."

One reason for subordinating the concept of respect for life is that people who support abortion rights fear that otherwise there could be restrictions on access to abortion. When the focus is on human dignity, and the human involved is a pregnant woman, her right to choose to terminate the pregnancy is upheld on the basis of upholding her dignity. If respect for life is also recognized as an equally important value, the claims of the fetus become much more central and a choice has to be made between the conflicting rights of the woman and the fetus. It's not so clear that the woman's right to dignity should prevail when the issue is framed this way.

Insights about what respect for human life requires in the context of the new reproductive technologies can come from diverse sources. For instance, Emile Durkheim, in his book *Suicide*,[17] refers to the belief in the inherent dignity and worth of human life as "the religion of humanity" and concludes that it is the only cohesive bond in a diverse and secular world. Durkheim regards this belief as the last one that "unites us as a human community and serves as the essential basis of our social and moral order." The French philosopher Paul Ricoeur sums up the same approach in a few simple but powerful words: something is owed to human beings simply due to the fact that they are human.[18] This "religion of human-ity" is almost certainly the non-negotiable minimum we need to form a viable human society — or at least one in which most of us would think it was worthwhile living. The question I want to address here is, What does respect for life require in the context of respect for human dignity?

Whether the concept of respect for life and that of dig-nity are compatible or in conflict can depend on which concept of human dignity we espouse. If humans are seen to have intrinsic dignity (that is, dignity simply because they are human), there is usually no conflict between respect for life and for the person's dignity — indeed, respecting their life is required in order to respect their human dignity and vice versa. Extrinsic dignity means that dignity is a matter of assessing the situation in which a person finds himself, whether the assessment is made by that person or by another. In other words, dignity is conferred on a person; it is not innate simply because one is human. The concept of extrinsic dignity is much more likely to result in a conflict between respect for life and for dignity. This occurs when upholding the person's dignity is seen to require that respect for life be breached — as in abortion or euthanasia. To put it another way, respecting the person's dignity is seen to require upholding their right to autonomy. A concept of extrinsic human dignity is closely linked to individualism, especially to upholding individuals' rights to autonomy. It is a relativist approach, in that we do not have dignity simply because we are human; whether we have dignity and what is required to uphold it all depends upon the circumstances in which we find ourselves.

Another way to look at dignity is as a concept used to establish and reflect a certain hierarchy of values. If your primary value is personal autonomy and self-determination, then dignity will be used to establish and reflect that by giving priority to those values. Likewise, if your primary value is respect for life, dignity will be used to give priority to that value. Societies based on intense individualism have moved from using the concept of human dignity to uphold a primary value of respect for life to using it to give priority to personal autonomy and self-determination.

In other words, the content of the concept of human dignity has been changed and, with that, the priority of values it establishes has changed — although, like the chicken and the egg, which change came first is unclear. Instead of dignity upholding respect for human life, human life that does not manifest characteristics of personal autonomy and self-determination is seen as undignified, and respect for dignity is seen as being implemented by eliminating that undignified life. More generally, if we equate dignity to autonomy, then limiting a person's autonomy infringes upon their dignity. This places us in the difficult situation of being forced to choose between infringing on people's dignity by limiting their rights to autonomy, or failing to protect others and society, including important societal values, by not doing so. Yet if we see our fullest experience of human dignity as including our relationships with others, including society, then protecting those relationships, which can require limiting personal autonomy, is dignity-enhancing, not dignity-limiting.

I suggest that the changes in the concept of dignity outlined above have often been deliberately employed as a "confusion strategy" — people do not understand the full import of what the changes mean. It is not enough to ask people what values they affirm but, more importantly, what values they are willing to negate. Often the values negated are not identified, sometimes intentionally, in order to promote a consensus that supports a certain outcome. We should have great concern when the values negated are respect for human life and the equality of all people — the inherent dignity and equality of everyone. Yet this is the end result of adopting an extrinsic concept of dignity and equating the content of the concept of dignity to that of autonomy.

To explore what respect for intrinsic human dignity would require in the context of new reproductive technologies, we can rephrase Ricoeur's principle: What do we owe to the human beings who would be affected by new reproductive technologies — in particular, what does respect for their intrinsic human dignity require that we *not* do to them? Since all humans must be seen as subjects, not objects, we must avoid using technologies in any way that detracts from humans being regarded or treated as objects. The obligations we owe to human beings include not to manufacture them; not to make them into objects or commodities; and to respect their right not to be designed by another human. A concept of extrinsic dignity entails few if any of these restrictions, largely because human dignity is not attributed to an embryo or fetus until, at the earliest, it is born alive and viable.

Some ethicists — for instance, Ruth Macklin — are now arguing that a concept of human dignity is useless.[19] That is true of a concept of extrinsic dignity, because it only affirms individuals' rights to autonomy, rights that already exist. It is not true, however, of a concept of intrinsic dignity. Unlike extrinsic dignity, intrinsic dignity establishes a base line of respect for persons *that is not negotiable*. Intrinsic dignity upholds the value of each person's equal worth, not primarily his or her autonomy. Extrinsic dignity focuses on maintaining respect for people's "actions, thoughts, concerns,"[20] which is respect for their exercise of autonomy. Intrinsic dignity focuses on respect for each and every person regardless of their characteristics — that is, respect for people themselves.

It is worth noting that the current debate around dignity is not limited to the ivory tower of academia. Starbucks is running a campaign called "The Way I See It." Starbucks claims that it has "always supported a good healthy discussion," and in the tradition of coffee houses that spark good conversations it has acquired a "collection of thoughts, opinions and expressions provided by notable figures," which it prints on its coffee cups to encourage good conversations amongst its customers. Here's what lawyer and author Wesley J. Smith wrote as quote number 127:

> The morality of the 21st century will depend on how we respond to this simple but profound question: Does every human life have equal moral value simply and merely because it is human? Answer yes, and we have a chance of achieving universal human rights. Answer no, and it means that we are merely another animal in the forest.

A powerful warning that this is no insignificant issue or choice on our parts.

The Link Between Respect for Life and Ethics

Respect for all life, in particular human life, is important not only in itself, but also because it is intimately linked to the foundations of ethics. Albert Schweitzer arrestingly articulated that connection in his book *Civilization and Ethics*, when he wrote:

> Ethics, too, are nothing but reverence for life. This is what gives me the fundamental principle of morality, namely, that good consists in maintaining, promoting, and enhancing life, and that destroying, injuring, and limiting life are evil.[21]

As Glenn Albrecht, an environmental philosopher-ethicist, argues, "[S]uch a broad perspective on ethics is easily universalized . . . [including,] into social and environmental contexts."[22] Albrecht describes with approval the "new organicists," environmental ethicists who see all life as a complex interrelated entity, where the "integration is not only material but ethical and possibly 'spiritual' as well (in the sense that the individual 'life spirit' can be strongly connected to a universal 'life spirit')." The "new organicists" believe that:

> The idea of man's autarchy can be only a delusion, a kind of schizoid withdrawal into a makebelieve world; in truth, there is no escaping the ecological matrix. Once they accept the simple scientific fact of interdependence, men and women can be taught to practice a liferevering ethic . . .[23]

And, as Albrecht points out, "a life respecting ethic is also a human respecting ethic."[24] But the converse is also true: A human-respecting ethic is also a life-respecting ethic, provided we see ourselves as part of the great web of life that must be respected in its entirety and not as the only form of life that deserves respect. So what is required for a human-life-respecting ethic in the context of the new reproductive technologies and genetics that, in combination, constitute the field of reprogenetics? Let's examine that question by looking at some of the ethical challenges this new technoscience raises, starting with the facts, because good facts are essential to good ethics.

What Has Changed in Human Reproduction?

To answer this question, we first need to look at the characteristics of human reproduction fifty years ago. Whether and when a child was conceived was largely a matter of chance — although, of course, one could eliminate chance by not engaging in sexual intercourse, or reduce it by much less effective contraception than is available today. A child was always conceived in a woman's body. Life was transmitted to the child through sexual reproduction. The genetic heritage the child received was determined by the natural recombination of the genes carried in the female parent's ovum and the male parent's sperm. Those genes were received by the child in their natural or unaltered state. The sex of the child was a matter of chance. The only outcome of the transmission of life was reproduction, whether or not that outcome was desired, or a failure to reproduce. There was no further purpose for transmitting human life by creating an embryo. And, with the abolition of slavery, human beings and human life were not for sale; they were, as the Napoleonic Code states, *hors de commerce*.

Every element in this list has now changed, thanks to new technological developments. When human life is conceived can now be controlled through contraception, especially oral contraceptives ("the pill"). The place of conception is no longer limited to the single option of a woman's body. In vitro fertilization (IVF) allows the creation of embryos outside the body of a woman in a petri dish or test tube. The transmission of human life is no longer limited to sexual reproduction: cloning is asexual replication, and in the future, embryos may be created from one ovum,[25] the union of two ova or two sperm, from "synthetic" gametes (sperm or ova) made from adults' stem cells, or possibly from the individual genes that make up a living human — that is, through synthetic biology. A baby with three genetic parents has already been born. An ovum from one woman was enucleated, leaving the mitochondrial DNA, and the nucleus of another woman's ovum was inserted. This procedure overcame the problem of the second woman's defective mitochondrial DNA. The "combined ovum" was then fertilized with the sperm of the second woman's husband to allow them to have a child. An embryo's genetic heritage could now be altered through genetic manipulation and germ-cell line intervention. The range of people affected by that altered heritage is now greatly broadened, in that genetic alterations can go beyond the immediate embryo. Altering an embryo's germ cells means that all future descendants of that embryo will be altered in the same way — unless, of course, those genes are re-altered.

The sex of a child is now open to choice by parents, or even others. Abortion is often supported with the mantra that "all children will be wanted children"; sex selection can be supported likewise: all children will be of the wanted sex. In many countries, the purpose in transmitting human life by creating an embryo is no longer only reproduction; embryos are also created for research or to be used as a source of stem cells for making therapeutic products, processes that necessarily involve killing the embryos. In other words, the transmission of human life for these purposes is undertaken with the primary intention of killing the life created. In Canada, the Assisted Human Reproduction Act of 2004[26] prohibits creating embryos other than for the purpose of having a child. Many researchers, lobby groups, and industries are calling for change to this prohibition. So-called "spare" embryos left over from IVF may be used for research or as a source of stem cells, provided certain conditions are fulfilled. And in many countries, although at least in theory not in Canada, gametes are sold and bought, as are embryos and fetuses for their organs and tissues or to use in research. Finally, commercial surrogate motherhood means women's uteruses are for rent. The chief executive of one Sydney, Australia fertility clinic summed it up this way: "In the future you will have sex for fun, but when you have babies, you'll have IVF."[27]

And what else might the future hold with respect to reprogenetic technologies? Gestation (when the fetus is in a woman's uterus) is the one situation where we are still dependent on "using a human," although whether that human must be a woman is now open to question. The successful delivery of a baby that developed outside her mother's uterus raises the possibility of gestation for men.[28] Using an animal to gestate a human fetus is prohibited under the Assisted Human Reproduction Act in Canada. We have not yet developed a safe and effective artificial uterus but research in this area is taking place, and when an artificial uterus, is developed — as seems likely — the whole process of human reproduction will be open to being carried out in a technoscience environment, rather than an intimate human one. We have no idea what impact this would have on the children brought into the world by these means, most importantly on the bonds between them and their parents and extended families. Moreover, these new reprogenetic technologies, especially in combination with changing views of marriage and parenthood (for instance, same-sex marriage and intentional single motherhood), constitute unprecedented challenges to children's rights with respect to their biological origins, knowing who their biological parents are, and the nature of the parenting they will receive.

We might get an idea of the scope of the possible changes and challenges by looking at what resulted from the creation of the Internet — although the effects of the Internet are likely to seem minor compared with the results of the complete technologization, and associated dehumanization, of human reproduction. The technologies that now make up the Internet had each been around for half a century before the Internet became a (virtual) reality: fax machines since the 1930s, modems and radio phones since the 1940s. It was only when we finally figured out how to connect communications and information technologies — how, for instance, to let one modem talk to another on the telephone and agree between themselves — that they had the massive impact on our world, including its culture and values, we have witnessed. This is even more likely to be true for the combined impact of reproductive and genetic technologies — that is, reprogenetics. In particular, these new technoscience possibilities bring us face to face with unprecedented questions about who we are, how we find meaning in life, and what respect for human life requires. Let's look at the last of these questions in more detail.

Respect for Human Life in Light of Reprogenetics

Reprogenetic technoscience means that we hold human life in the palm of our collective hand in a way that no one before us has ever done. As a result, our respect for life is challenged in unprecedented ways. We are the first people to face these challenges, because no humans before us were able to intervene and affect life in the ways we now can. So, what is required of us?

To begin, we now need to consider the ethical requirements of respect for human life in at least five ways — two old ways and three new ones. We have long recognized the need to respect each individual life, and human life in general, at the societal level. These are the old ways. But we now need such respect in three new ways: First, with the development of in vitro fertilization (IVF), we need to consider what respect for the earliest form of human life, human embryos, requires, because they can now exist outside a woman's body. Second, we must consider what is needed if we are to show respect for the transmission of human life, because we can now transmit human life in unprecedented ways for unprecedented purposes. And third, we must consider what is required for respect for the essence of human life, the human germ-cell line, the genes passed on from generation to generation, because they can now be manipulated.

Traditional Respect for Human Life

I've already remarked that respect for human life has always required both respect for each individual life and respect for human life in general. However, even this traditional respect is now being challenged by new technologies such as preimplantation genetic diagnosis (PGD) and prenatal screening.

Individual parents-to-be are screening their embryos and fetuses for genetic and developmental problems and choosing to discard embryos or to abort fetuses that are genetically or developmentally "defective." Whatever our view of the ethics of these decisions at the individual level, at a societal level they might have the effect of wiping out certain groups of people, such as Down's syndrome children, achondroplastic (dwarf) children, or those who are profoundly deaf or manic-depressive (those with bipolar disorder). Apart from a failure to respect the lives of the individuals involved, this would eliminate the special gifts these people bring to society. And what other groups would be reduced in number? In some countries, female embryos or fetuses are identified and eliminated. And if gay genes are identified, as seems likely for male homosexuality,[29] a justified fear is that gay people would be reduced in number. In short, the cumulative effect of individual decision-making is resulting in a situation that would never be tolerated as public policy.

We must directly and honestly address the question: are we creating a "new eugenics" with our use of reprogenetic technologies? People who want to avoid or finesse this question will argue that individual choice about the nature of one's child is not a eugenic decision. Rather, eugenics is practised only when a choice is made about a group or class of people, or by someone who is not the future parent. But this is sophistry.

And what might history have to tell us about eugenics? Speaking of the 1920s and 1930s eugenics movement, author Heather Menzies says, "[M]any scientists had already distanced themselves from the determinism of genetic agency by the 1930s when eugenicists took it up with notions of some people being fit for reproduction and others not." Paraphrase Menzies slightly by replacing the word "reproduction" with the word "life," and what she says of the 1930s might ring true today: Many people had already distanced themselves from pure genetic determinism by the early 2000s when, through their use of genetic technologies, prospective parents, geneticists, and, indirectly, governments took it up with notions of some people being fit for life and others not.

Menzies continues: "All the more reason to wonder at the seeming persistence of this notion [of genetic determinism] today. Although now, if this is eugenics, it's not couched in totalitarian population control, but as private consumer choice. As [evolutionary biologist Michael] Rose spelled out in a 1999 *Scientific American* article, 'people are going to have to spend a very significant fraction of their disposable income on whatever gene-related products emerge. It's a privatized form of eugenics, domesticated by the marketplace and its tireless capacity for dreams.'"[30]

Such uses of reprogenetic technology and prenatal screening have even wider effects for society and for important values apart from respect for life. These procedures involve treating the embryo or fetus as an object — if it is not of acceptable quality, or of the "right" sex or sexual orientation, it will be discarded. This, in turn, affects the role of the parent-child bond in establishing important societal values. Our understanding of parental love — as the parents' unconditional acceptance of, and love for, the child born to them simply because the child is *their child* — is drastically changed. The parents' love becomes conditional on the child having certain characteristics and not having others. This is a fundamental change in the shared morality and values on which society has traditionally rested.

Another issue that is currently challenging our ideas of respect for human life is as old as the human race — that of euthanasia and physician-assisted suicide. This is no accident. The "new eugenics" and euthanasia share many characteristics. The two great events of each and every human life, birth and death, have always been the focuses of our most important shared values as a society. We have lost our sense of mystery and reverence in relation to both and replaced those senses with anxiety and fear — fear of suffering and loss, whether the cause is the imperfect child or our own failing body. In both cases, we take control and eliminate the perceived cause.[31]

I'd like to turn now to the three new ways in which respect for human life is required: for the earliest stage of human life, human embryos; for the transmission of human life; and for the essence of human life — the human germ-cell line. The order in which I address these matters reflects the chronological order in which we faced them as a result of developments in reproductive and genetic technologies.

Respect for In Vitro Human Embryos

With the advent of in vitro fertilization (IVF) in the late 1970s, for the first time we were faced with human embryos conceived outside the body of a woman — we had "test tube babies." In the early days of IVF, one of the world's leading team of scientists and physicians were at Monash University in Melbourne, Australia. I spent a six-month sabbatical there, looking at the ethical and legal issues their work was raising. One day I was in the operating room after a patient had been prepared for transfer of IVF embryos into her uterus. She was lying on the operating table covered in white drapes, with her feet in stirrups. Her husband, dressed in sterile gown and cap (as we all were), was at the head of the table holding her hand. Obstetrician-gynecologist Dr. Carl Wood drew up the embryos from the petri dish into the long, thin, flexible tube he would insert through her cervix to deposit the embryos in her uterus. He said, "Now, Mrs. Smith, we are going to put in the embryos." She responded, "Just a minute, doctor." She paused. "Could we please see our babies before you do that?" Dr. Wood walked to the head of the table, showed the woman and her husband the tube, which looked as though it had a small amount of clear water in it, and pointed to the lower third of it. "You can't see them, but that's where they are," he said. Still holding hands, the woman and her husband stared at the tube and then turned to each other, exchanging the radiant smiles one sees on parents' faces moments after the birth of their baby. For this couple, their "babies" had come into the world.

IVF confronts us with the question: what does respect for in vitro human embryos require? Although some people object to any creation of embryos outside a woman's

body, most accept that it is ethical to use IVF for the purpose of having a child. But it is one thing to argue the
ethics of using IVF for that purpose, quite another when
IVF embryos are created for research or to use as the
source of stem cells to make therapeutic products that
benefit the rest of us. I will get to the ethics of transmission of life for these purposes shortly, but here I want to
ask: What respect must we pay to IVF embryos, in themselves, once they exist? Are human embryos human
beings or human products? Is using an embryo as an
object, commodity, or product ethical? Our answers
depend on the respect owed to the human embryo, and
that respect is linked to the embryo's moral status.

There are three views on the moral status of a human
embryo, representing a continuum from permissiveness to
prohibition with respect to what it is ethical to do to it. The
first, most permissive, view sees no reason to respect the
human embryo. In this view, the human embryo has *no
moral status* but is equivalent to, say, a skin cell. Whatever
may ethically be done to a skin cell may be done to a
human embryo. Indeed, people supporting the use of
embryos for therapeutic or research purposes try to avoid
the word embryo, describing it as just "a small clump of
cells,"[32] and adding words such as "the size of the head of
a pin" and "like any other cells." They deny that life
begins at conception, and therefore that destruction of
human life is involved. They emphasize the scientific
advancement, and therapeutic and economic benefits,
promised by creating human embryos for research and the
harms and losses of prohibiting it, as Canadian law does.

The second view is more restrictive than the first and acknowledges that some respect is owed to the human embryo. The position of people who share this view is that the *human embryo has moral status and deserves respect, but not (yet) the same respect as the rest of us*. Therefore, the embryo may be used in ways that would not be ethically acceptable if applied to the rest of us — it is *potential* human life.

The third, most restrictive and respectful, view is that the human embryo is the *earliest stage of each human life and as such has the same moral status as the rest of us* — we are all ex-embryos. Therefore, the embryo's life must be respected and it must not be used simply as a product or a means to an end — it is human life *with potential*. As is true for all of us until we die, its life is a life in progress, and the embryo is in the process of becoming all that it can be. If we are in any doubt as to the respect owed to human embryos, we should treat them with full respect.

Currently, Canadian law, as promulgated in the Assisted Human Reproduction Act, adopts the second position. Embryos may only be created with the intention that they will be used to have a child through IVF; they must not be created for research. Those "leftover" from IVF — so-called "spare" embryos — may be used for research where the gamete donors give fully informed consent, and the research is important and cannot be carried out without using embryos. This approach is sometimes justified ethically on the basis of the "nothing's lost" concept: because the embryos would die anyway, nothing's lost in using them for research. That may be true for an individual embryo that would be allowed to die, but there is a loss of respect for the earliest form of human life in using it for research and destroying it in doing so. Whether that loss matters in itself depends upon one's views about the embryo. But it might also matter when we consider respect for life in general.

As we look at respect for human embryos in vitro, we can also examine the issue of sex selection — in particular, the societal concerns it raises. In making decisions about whether to allow or prohibit the use of sex-selection technology, we must look beyond the personal preferences of people who want a child only of a certain sex and ask what impact such choices would have on society and its values, especially in the more distant future. Recent reports on the millions of missing girls in the world as a result of female feticide in countries such as China and India raise serious concerns about the effects that the gender imbalance will have in those countries.[33] In dealing with such realities, we must also consider the moral risks involved, not just the physical risks. There is a universe of difference between parents who want a child only if it comes into the world satisfying specific criteria for quality or sex, and parents welcoming the child they beget in a spirit of humility and with unconditional love, which they understand as the primary characteristic of the parent-child bond.

These two radically contrasting attitudes reflect diametrically opposed values, and we must not turn a blind eye to the fact that our choice for one approach over the other will necessarily establish corresponding societal values. We should also recognize that sometimes saying no, especially to individuals who desperately want something and plead to be allowed to have it, is much harder, and requires more courage, than saying yes — especially when it involves something as seemingly innocuous, at first glance, as a family with three boys wanting a girl.

Whether sex-selection should be altogether prohibited is not clear ethically. Discarding embryos or aborting fetuses on the basis that they are the "wrong" sex should be seen as unethical. There is a major ethical difference, however, between choosing or discarding human gametes (sperm or ova) and choosing or discarding human embryos or fetuses. The latter are lives-in-being, the former are not. Consequently, using sperm-separation technology and then inseminating ova with either only X sperm or only Y sperm in order to conceive a female or male embryo, respectively, should not be totally prohibited, although the reason for sex selection does matter ethically. In particular, if there were a medical reason to avoid a child of a certain sex — for instance, a serious genetic disease that only affects boys — such a process would, in my view, be ethically acceptable. Such a stance is reflected in the Canadian Assisted Human Reproduction Act. It prohibits sex selection except for sound medical reasons.

Respect for the Transmission of Human Life

The next question we face is, What does respect for the transmission of human life require of us? This can be broken into three sub-questions: What is required if we are to show the necessary respect for life in how life is transmitted — that is, what limits does respect for life place on the mode of the transmission of life? What is required if we are to show the necessary respect for life from the perspective of the intention with which we transmit life — that is, what limits does respect for life place on what we intend to do to the life created? And, what is required if we are to show the necessary respect for life in relation to the purpose for which life is transmitted?

In the past, the only mode of transmission was sexual reproduction. New modes of transmission include cloning (asexual replication) and having more than two genetic parents. Future modes could include making embryos — transmitting human life — by combining two ova or two sperm (so two men or two women could have their own shared baby) or by creating "synthetic" gametes (sperm or ova) made from adults' stem cells (which could be used by same-sex couples, or opposite-sex ones when one person is infertile, or would allow one person to become both the "mother" and "father" of their own baby without the baby being a clone). We should regard transmitting human life in these ways as unethical, both from the standpoint of respect for the transmission of human life itself and from the perspective of the rights and claims of the resulting child.

The question of whether gametes should be donated and, if so, under what conditions, also raises ethical issues, not least in relation to children's rights to know their genetic identity — to know through whom life travelled down the generations to them. And the source of donated gametes can raise ethical problems — for instance, using ova recovered from an aborted fetus is, in my view, itself unethical, and it is unethical for a child to be born to a mother who "never existed" in the sense of being born. Likewise, creating a child from the gametes of a dead donor should be considered unethical. I believe that to intentionally bring a child into the world knowing that it will never know its biological parent or parents is wrong.

Let's look at cloning, which is often sub-classified into "reproductive cloning" — cloning with the intention of having a child, and "therapeutic cloning" — creating embryos to use them to make therapeutic products for the rest of us (that is, setting up a "human embryo manufacturing plant). Most people — but not all, by any means — believe that it is inherently wrong to transmit human life by cloning, with the intention that a child should result. I would go further. I believe that it is inherently wrong to transmit life, intending that a child should result, other than by sexual reproduction through the union of the natural ovum from one identified, living, adult woman and the natural sperm from one identified, living, adult man. Moreover, even using a utilitarian analysis, any benefits provided by modes of transmission other than sexual reproduction are far outweighed by the risks and harms — not only to the resulting child, including but not limited to physical risks, but also to our sense of what it means to be human, how we find our own identity and meaning in life, and to the meaning we attach to passing on human life to the next generation in the way it was passed on to us.

The related technologies of therapeutic cloning and human embryo stem-cell research raise ethical issues about the intention with which life is transmitted, and the purpose for which it is done. The use for research of so-called "spare" embryos "leftover" from IVF is itself ethically controversial. The creation of embryos for use in research or to make therapeutic products (whether through sexual reproduction or cloning) raises ethical issues, however, that go beyond those issues. In contrast to IVF, where the intention is to have a baby, creating embryos for research or cloning them to make therapeutic products (both are crimes in Canada under the Assisted Human Reproduction Act) involves transmitting human life with no intention of giving the embryo any chance to live — indeed, with the intention of killing it. Furthermore, creating an embryo for the sole purpose of making therapeutic products is to use it as an object. And once a technology that uses embryos is developed, the transmission of human life is undertaken for commercial goals. As this example demonstrates, reprogenetics brings into question our most intimate connections as humans to other humans — to those to whom we give life itself.

As discussed previously, cloning is almost universally seen as unethical if the intention is to produce a child. But advocates of therapeutic cloning argue that this is different from reproductive cloning. Both, however, offend the requirements of respect for the mode of transmission of human life, as would other technologies on the scientific horizon for transmitting human life other than by the union of a natural sperm and a natural ovum. Most

recently, there have been efforts to create human embryonic stem cells without creating an embryo in order to
avoid ethical problems. We should hope that such a solution can be developed. But deliberately creating a
"disabled" embryo — one that has no potential for development — raises its own ethical problems and is not such
a solution.

To regard activities such as the making of embryos for
use as products — and in doing so, killing them — as ethical rests on an assumption that we own life, and
therefore can treat it as we wish; we have a right to
dominion over it. The contrasting view is that we are
holding life on trust for present and future generations in
ways no other humans ever have held it. If we believe
this, then we must ask what such a belief requires that we
not do with our new technoscience. We would do well to
listen to the philosopher Jürgen Habermas in answering
that question. He says that respect for what he calls "pre-
personal human life" is necessary to maintain our ethical
understanding of what it means to be human, and that
there is a long-established, widely shared, deep moral
intuition that human embryos are not just things.[34] Interestingly, recent research strongly supports the existence
of this intuition. This research shows the personal way in
which people relate to their stored IVF embryos and the
great emotional difficulty they have in deciding what
should happen to them.[35] Creating embryos for research
and therapeutic cloning necessarily means that we treat
the transmission of life as a commodity manufacturing
process, and embryos as objects. Doing so breaches the

respect the moral intuition that embryos are not just things demands of us. We undertake such acts at our ethical peril.

Respect for the Human Germ-cell Line

Yet another question we are the first humans to face is: What does respect for the essence of human life — the human germ-cell line, or the genes that are passed on from generation to generation — require of us? These genes are the product of around 850 million years of evolution — whether we believe that evolution occurred through natural selection or also involved intelligent design. We can now change that evolution in nanoseconds. What must we do, what may we do, and what must we not do to the germ-cell line? In changing an embryo's germ-cell line, we change not only that embryo, but also all of its descendants in like manner. Is it ever acceptable to do that?

Another way to ask the same question is: What is required of us by the obligation to hold the human germ-cell line on trust for future generations as the common heritage of humankind? Does it mean, as many people believe, that intentional alteration of it is never justified? What if we could eliminate a horrible disease by changing just one gene, and we knew it was reasonably safe to do that? Do we object to intentionally altering the human germ-cell line because we believe that it is inherently wrong to do so — that is, a purpose of doing good can never be a justification for interfering with it? If so, then we must never intervene.

Or do we believe that some interventions might be justifiable — that is, it is not inherently wrong to intervene on the human germ-cell line, but intervening is not currently justifiable because it is too dangerous? One aspect of that danger is the unpredictability of the effects of eliminating or changing a single gene. Initially scientists believed that one gene coded for one protein in the human body — they knew there were 100,000 to 130,000 proteins, so they expected to find the same number of genes. Now they believe that we probably have about 30,000 to 32,000 genes. One gene can code for several proteins — perhaps in some cases up to 1,000 — depending on which sections of the gene are active. This multiple-coding capacity is called pleiotropy. Moreover, whether a gene functions and, if so, how can depend on its interactions with other genes and with the environment. So knocking out or altering a particular gene would have highly unpredictable effects.

Or do we fear altering the human germ-cell line because, once intervention is allowed, no matter how much suffering we might eliminate, we could not control the range of interventions that would occur? Do we envision a future in which many interventions would be at best frivolous, while others, such as intentional disenhancement of the intelligence of certain embryos or making others hyper-aggressive (for instance, to breed soldiers, a topic I raised previously) would be profoundly, ethically unacceptable?

Genetic manipulation of human embryos, whether to enhance or disenhance them, destroys the essence of their humanness and, ultimately, the essence of the humanness of all of us. Genetic manipulation interferes with the intrinsic being of a person — with their very "self." As philosopher Søren Kierkegaard puts it, the designed person is not free to fully become themselves, which is the essence of freedom. The power to fully become oneself requires that the person has non-contingent origins — they need to have a sense that they can go back and start again to remake or actualize their very self, and in order to have that they must not be preprogrammed or designed by another. As Jürgen Habermas argues, designed persons no longer can own themselves, which is necessary to make their being and their lives fully their own — they are not free in their intrinsic being, and they are not equal to their designer. This affects the humanness of all of us because, first, we would all be complicit in such manipulation by not prohibiting it. And second, because tampering with some people's origins destroys a necessary condition for establishing a moral base for a secular society — that all people must be free from others' interference in their intrinsic being, if they are to have the capacity to take part in the human interaction from which a shared morality arises.

The injustice of one generation imposing its will over another generation (if the first generation designs its own children) would result in losses that have implications far beyond those directly affected. The use of these technologies by one generation challenges the basic human rights of equality and freedom of future generations. And because the liberty and equality of all citizens is at the heart of societal institutions and of values such as democracy and liberalism, to create people who are neither free nor equal undermines those institutions and values.

New Rights for Children

So far I have looked at the ethics of the new reproductive technologies (NRTS) in terms of their immediate use. But these technologies result in children being born. What do we owe those children ethically? This question has been largely ignored. Our ethical focus on NRTS has been almost entirely on adults' rights to access these technologies, and their use of them to found a family. But as the first cohort of children born as a result of NRTS reaches adulthood, they are changing our focus. What are their rights with respect to the nature of their genetic heritage and to knowledge of what that heritage is? I will briefly mention some of the issues that are currently being debated around the world as these donor-conceived adults, as they call themselves, connect with one another largely through the Internet.

Donor-conceived and adopted children tell us that they wonder: Do I have siblings or cousins? Who are they? What are they like? Are they "like me"? What could I learn about myself from them? These questions raise the issue of how our blood relatives help each of us to establish our human identity. Humans identify closely with their close genetic family, and it seems that we also identify with traits in our family members that we like (and we try to develop the same ones in ourselves), and that we dislike (and vow not to be like that — the positive power of negative identification).[36]

The issue of children's rights to know their genetic identity or the nature of their genetic origins arises, in one way or another, in the contexts of adoption, the use of new reproductive technologies, and same-sex marriage. The connection among these contexts is that they all unlink child-parent biological bonds. Each context raises one or more of three important issues: children's right to know the identity of their biological parents; children's right to both a mother and a father, preferably their own biological parents; and children's right to come into being with genetic origins that have not been tampered with.

Children's Rights to Know the Identity of their Biological Parents

It is one matter for children not to know their genetic identity as a result of unintended circumstances. It is quite another matter to deliberately destroy children's links to their biological parents, and especially for society to be complicit in this destruction. It is now being widely recognized that adopted children have the right to know who their biological parents are whenever possible, and legislation establishing that right has become the norm. The same right is increasingly being accorded to children born through gamete (sperm or ovum) donation. For instance, the United Kingdom has recently passed laws giving children this right at eighteen years of age.

The impact of NRTs on children born through their use, other than that on their physical health, has been largely ignored; it has been readily assumed that no major ethical or other problems arise in creating children from donated gametes, and that opposition to the creation of these children is almost entirely based on religious beliefs. Such assumptions have been dramatically challenged in the last two years as the first people born through the use of these technologies reach adulthood, become activists, and call for change. They describe powerful feelings of loss of identity through not knowing one or both biological parents and their wider biological families, and describe themselves as "genetic orphans."[37] They ask, How could anyone think they had the right to do this to me? We can read a striking imaginary account of the power of this longing in Kazuo Ishiguro's book *Never Let Me Go*.[38] It deals with children created through cloning to serve as organ donors to those who commissioned their creation.

Ethics, human rights, and international law — as well as considerations such as the health and well-being of adopted and donor-conceived children — all require that children have access to information regarding their biological parents. And it is not just these children who have this right, but their future descendants as well. Children deprived of knowledge of their genetic identity — and their descendants — are harmed physically and psychologically. Respect for children's rights in these regards requires that the law should prohibit anonymous sperm and ova donation, establish a donor registry, and recognize children's rights to know their biological parents and, thereby, their own biological identity. It is a further question whether gamete donation itself is ethically acceptable. Many of us have come to accept that it should be made available to couples who do not regard it as immoral. (Whether it should be available to same-sex couples, or single women, is a much more contentious issue.) But some donor-conceived adults are arguing that we have been wrong as a society in allowing gamete donation.

Children's Rights to Both a Mother and a Father

When marriage is limited to the union of a man and a woman, it establishes as the norm children's rights to both a mother and a father, preferably their own biological parents, and to be reared by them, unless there are good reasons to the contrary in the "best interests" of a particular child. Adoption is an exception of this kind. As discussed previously, same-sex marriage unavoidably nullifies this right for all children, not just those brought into same-sex marriages. It does so because marriage can no longer establish as the norm on which the family is based the natural, inherently procreative relationship between a man and a woman, and therefore can no longer establish the rights of children to both a mother and a father. The Canadian Civil Marriage Act[39] expressly recognizes and implements that change by redefining parenthood in various federal acts from natural (or biological) parenthood to legal (and social) parenthood.[40] As also explained previously, under international and national law, the right to marry is twofold — the right to marry *and* to found a family. This means that children in the families of same-sex spouses who exercise their right to found a family will have same-sex parents, not a mother and a father. The same issue of children's rights to both a mother and a father is raised by society's involvement in intentionally creating single-parent households, for example, by requiring that single women be given access to artificial insemination.

The debate on legalizing same-sex marriage in Canada focused almost entirely on adults and their right not to be discriminated against on the basis of their sexual orientation. The conflicting claims, rights, and needs of children were barely mentioned. It's worth noting here that legally recognizing civil unions, unlike the recognition of same-sex marriage, does not negate children's right to both a mother and a father and, I propose, represents the most ethical compromise between respect for the rights of homosexual people and those of children.

Children's Rights to be Born from Natural Biological Origins

It's now been more than twenty-five years since Louise Brown, the first "test tube baby," ushered in the brave new world opened up by NRTs. Current advances in NRTs make it necessary to formulate new rights for children in relation to their biological origins that would have been unimaginable until very recently. Let me explain the components of these rights in more detail.

First, children have a right to be born with a natural biological heritage and from natural biological origins — that is, to have untampered-with biological origins — in particular, to be conceived from one untampered-with, natural sperm from an identified and living adult man and one, untampered-with, natural ovum from an identified and living adult woman. A right to a natural biological heritage or a definition of the term *biological origins* was not necessary in the past, because there was no way that this right could be breached and the term *biological origins* could have only one meaning — the in vivo union of one man's sperm and one woman's ovum. The cloning of adult animals and the possibility of cloning adult humans showed us that is unlikely to remain true, and more recent scientific developments reinforce that message.

As I mentioned previously, it is theoretically possible to create an embryo with the genetic heritage of two women or two men — by making a sperm or ovum from one of the adult's stem cells and using a natural gamete from the other person; or by making an "ovum" from an enucleated egg fused with a sperm and fertilizing it with another sperm; or perhaps by using two ova. This would allow a same-sex couple to have their "own genetically shared baby." Likewise, a sterile opposite-sex couple might seek to use the same technology to have their "own shared baby." By law in Canada, both opposite-sex and same-sex married couples now have a right to found a family. Couples could argue that to prohibit such means of doing so would be unconstitutional discrimination, the former on the basis of physical disability (courts have recognized infertility as such) and the latter on the basis of sexual orientation, because using these technologies is the only way these infertile opposite-sex or same-sex couples can have their "own" babies. Therefore, it is not super-fluous to add the words *man* and *woman* in defining children's rights to natural biological origins, rather than simply referring to sperm and ova. And requiring that the sperm and ovum be "natural" excludes the possibility of opposite-sex infertile couples using this technology.

Insisting that gametes come from adults would pre-empt the use of gametes from aborted fetuses; it thereby prevents children being born whose biological parents were never born. The requirement that the donors be living excludes the use of gametes for *post mortem* concep-tion. The right to bear children should not include the right to deny children at least the chance, when being conceived, of meeting their biological parents. Conceiv-ing children with gametes from a dead donor, as an Australian court recently authorized,[41] denies them this opportunity. In that case, the judge considered only the rights and wishes of the adults involved.

A Shared Ethics Regarding the Nature of Children's Rights

Perhaps most of us might agree on these requirements regarding new rights for children, which means we might be able to find a shared ethics in these regards. We might agree that it is prima facie harmful to children to create them without a natural biological heritage, without the right to know their biological origins, or knowing that their biological parent was never born or is dead. In that case, whether we come from a principled base or from a perspective of ethical relativism, we could agree that doing so is unethical — that is, we could find a shared ethics.

All these rights of children are of the same basic ethical nature — obligations of non-malfeasance, that is, obligations to *first do no harm*. Consequently, as a society, we have obligations to ensure respect for these rights of children. It is one matter, ethically, not to interfere with people's rights of privacy and self-determination, especially in an area as intimate and personal as reproduction. It is quite another matter for society to become complicit in intentionally depriving children of their right to know and have contact with their biological parents and wider family, or their right to be born from natural biological origins. When society approves or funds procedures that can deprive children of these rights and, arguably, when it fails to protect such rights of children — for instance, by failing to enact protective legislation — society becomes complicit in the breaches of rights that ensue. Those obligations extend also to future generations. We should clearly recognize that any genetic procedure that will turn out to be harmful to the future child or to a future generation, or contrary to their interests, is morally unacceptable and should be prohibited.

I want to make it clear that in recommending we enact law to safeguard the rights of children, I in no way want to detract from the important principle that these are natural rights of the human person, and therefore their existence does not depend on their being enacted in law. Each of these rights is constitutive of the human person's self-identity; they are fundamental human rights — arguably the most fundamental — which cannot be denied by others or the state, even in the interests of those who seek the prerogative to bear children without these rights. In short, the right to bear children is much more accurately described as the right not to be prevented from, or interfered with in, bearing children through natural reproduction — a negative content right. That right does not include a positive content right to bear children in any way one wants and to have assistance, especially society's assistance, in doing so. In particular, it certainly does not include any right to bear children who will be denied their rights to be born from natural biological origins and to know their biological identity.

Knowing who our close biological relatives are and relating to them is central to how we form our human identity, relate to others and the world, and find meaning in life. Children — and their descendants — who don't know their genetic origins cannot sense themselves as embedded in a web of people, past, present and future, through whom they can trace the thread of life's passage down the generations to them. As far as we know, humans are the only animals who experience genetic relationships as integral to their sense of themselves. We are learning now that eliminating that experience is harmful to children, biological parents, families, and society. We can only imagine how much more damage might be done to a child born not from the union of a natural sperm and a natural ovum, but from "gametes" constructed through biotechnology.

• • •

Some people hold a "gene machine" view of human life — that we are nothing more than complex biological machines. Others regard human life as having intrinsic and not just instrumental value. Those who share the latter view see human life as unique, something special or "more" than the life other animals have — a "more" I try to capture in the term *human spirit*. We who hold an "intrinsic value" view of human life believe that we must be just as concerned about societal values as individual rights, and about how individual choices affect societal values. Nowhere are these choices more important for individuals and society alike than in upholding, or not, respect for life — in particular, when passing life on to our descendants.

It is therefore essential that we understand the implications of choosing the values that will govern the new reprogenetic technoscience. We must consider much more than the immediate medical and scientific benefits we hope for, or the thrill of the scientific discoveries we might make. Our choices in these matters and the values they uphold or reject go to the heart of what it means to be human. As a result, they will affect how we bond to one another as humans in our most intimate relationships — in particular, how we bond to the person with whom we transmit life to our children, bond to those children, find meaning in life, and see the essence of our humanness. These deeply important and intangible human realities are not indestructible. Indeed, they can be very fragile. We must choose, wisely and courageously, after full, open, and honest consideration of the ethics of our choices — both what we will do and, even more importantly, what we will not do with reprogenetic technoscience. And we must consider what roles a presumption in favour of the natural and concepts of respect for life, for intrinsic human dignity, for the natural — especially regarding human nature — and of the secular sacred might play in helping us to make wise choices.

IV

FROM *HOMO SAPIENS* TO *TECHNO SAPIENS*:

PROTECTING THE ESSENCE OF BEING HUMAN

As HUMANS, WE'RE both part of nature and part beyond nature — in our human spirit, our longing for transcendence and transformation. Our search for ethics can be seen as the marker of that duality, in that it is called into existence by the tension between those two parts, and its task is to accommodate them when they conflict. Such conflict is likely to become a more frequent occurrence as we gain power to change ourselves and our nature through the new technoscience. Ethics is an ongoing, dynamic process, not a checklist of dos and don'ts. Our search for it is an essential characteristic of the "beyond-nature" part of ourselves, an essential characteristic of our humanness. It is what distinguishes us from all other living beings.

Traditionally we protected the beyond-nature part of ourselves through a concept of the sacred, or in our contemporary societies, the secular sacred. This explains why those of us who see humans as having only a nature part, and who reject any beyond-nature part, have no need or use for a concept of the sacred. But protecting the beyond-nature part of us also requires protecting the nature part of us. The sacred intimately links the nature and beyond-nature parts of us in that it protects both. When we have two parts, we must either live simultaneously in two sep-arate silos — the Cartesian mind-body split — or we must somehow integrate the two parts. That is, we must deal with a more complex situation than if we were just a uni-tary whole. Ethics might be our contemporary anti-Cartesian instrument, a way to implement the theory of an integrated whole in relation to ourselves, a way to integrate the most intimate, foundational core of our nature; that is, ethics may be a way to fully integrate our-selves. The goal of integration is, once again, a permanently ongoing process, not an endpoint.

Theologian William May says our body does three things: it presents the world to us; it acts as our presence to the entire universe — in that if the body breaks, our personhood is threatened or disintegrates; and it is what relates to others.[1] How might interventions on our bodies — interventions that the new technoscience makes possi-ble — affect those functions? First, let's take a brief look at some possibilities opened up by recent scientific advances.

The Science

I've already described how we can now create embryos in vitro, choose the sex of our children, screen these children as embryos or fetuses for genetic diseases, and make an embryo from three genetic parents. In the future, reprogenetics will allow us to design our children and their children; clone ourselves; and make babies from two sperm or two ova, from synthetic gametes (sperm or ova) made from adults' stem cells, and from more than three genetic parents. I explained how essential it is that we ask ourselves: Are these ethically acceptable courses of conduct?

Even old "medical miracles" can raise this question in new ways. Scientific breakthroughs such as organ transplantation that we saw as world-shattering when they emerged, but have since become routine, can still challenge us ethically. To give an example: Partial face transplants have already been successfully undertaken. However, plans to perform the first total human-face transplant raise many more ethical issues. Is a person's general consent to the use of their organs and tissues for transplantation sufficient to authorize use of that person's face? And even if there is an express consent to such use by the donor before death, what if relatives of the donor object that they will be harmed by "seeing" their dead loved one in their community? Furthermore, what are the effects on the person receiving the transplant? Visible transplants have a different psychological effect on recipients than non-visible ones. And a face transplant magnifies that effect because the face reflects our personality and identity. What does the recipient experience when possessing someone else's face? Does he or she have a crisis of identity?[2] And even if we allowed total face transplants for medical reasons (such as horrific scar-ring), what about undertaking the procedure for cosmetic reasons, or to "disappear" so that your family can collect on an insurance policy, or to conceal your identity as a criminal?

As avant-garde as such interventions seem, there are others that are even more startling. For instance, we have discovered that ninety-eight percent of the genes that make up the human genome and the chimpanzee genome are the same. Let's assume these genes function in the same way in each species (they might not). What would happen if we replaced the two percent of the genes in the chimpanzee genome that differ from human ones with the relevant human genes? Would we create a child that has a *human phenotype* — he or she looks like any other human — but has a ninety-eight percent *chimpanzee genome*? What is this creature: a human, a chimpanzee, or neither? (Our most recent discoveries about the immensely complex way in which a genome functions makes the last possibility — that the creature would be something different from either human or chimp — a real probability.[3]) Or is it the two percent that matters? Is this creature truly human because it has the crucial human two percent? Does that two percent give humans their consciousness, language abilities, and powers of reasoning?

Never-before-possible human-animal (chimera) and human-machine (cyborg) combinations raise profound ethical questions. At present, we strongly reject human-animal combinations as immoral and unethical except when we use "minimalist" techniques, such as putting human-complement genes into pig embryos (apart from having safety concerns, many people accept this). In this instance, the human genes are inserted to prevent immediate rejection of the pigs' organs when they are used for transplantation into humans — that is, xenotransplantation, or transplantation across species. In contrast, recent proposals in the United States to create human-mouse hybrid embryos for research purposes caused an outcry, and resulted in statements by researchers, not usually regarded as conservative in their views, saying that to do so was unethical. Reports in newspapers that the procedure could result in a mouse with some level of human consciousness (or, one assumes, vice versa) explained the deep level of ethical concern.

Because they are more familiar to us through modern medical technology, human-machine combinations might, at first glance, seem less ethically problematic and threatening than human-animal combinations. But this assumption might prove to be untrue. In the section that follows, I want to explore the beliefs of people who style themselves "transhumanists" and who are predicting a posthuman future in which humans will be redesigned through technology to become cyborgs. According to transhumanists, the physical, mental, emotional, and even moral capacities of cyborgs will far outstrip those of unmodified humans æ except, they fail to note, the capacity of cyborgs to be human. Moreover, the acceptance of human-machine combinations could also lead to acceptance of human-animal combinations, if the values we choose to govern human-nonhuman combinations are to be consistent. It is not difficult to see why we would need ethics to guide this science.

Human Identity and Robots

Rodney Brooks, the scientist who heads the artificial intelligence laboratory at the Massachusetts Institute of Technology, describes in his book *Flesh and Machines*[4] a sliding scale of human reactions to other creatures. He starts with our reaction to other humans, who we see as being like ourselves and, as such, deserving of respect. He then moves to chimpanzees; to dogs, cats, and horses; to rats and mice; to worms; and to one-celled organisms. He argues that we respond to and respect these life forms at decreasing levels of intensity along that spectrum. He does not cite Princeton philosopher Peter Singer,[5] who argues that it is *speciesism* — wrongful discrimination against other species — to believe humans deserve special respect — a kind of respect that we do not give to other animals. However, Brooks, like Singer, says that humans are not special in any relevant sense, and therefore there is only a difference in degree, not a difference in kind, between the respect we give other humans and that we give the animals "nearest" to us on the spectrum. According to Brooks, that's as it should be.

Brooks points out that we see these other living entities as "beings," though not ones identical to ourselves. He then discusses whether robots could ever be regarded as "beings." He describes how students in his artificial intelligence laboratory, even those who have built robots and therefore would be most appreciative of robots' technological base, are disturbed by robots when they are controlled by someone other than themselves — especially when that person is hidden — and the robots seem to react in a humanlike way to circumstances in the laboratory or to the students. These reactions are likely to become more common as more sophisticated technologies — such as those involved in making humanlike skin for robots — are developed. Note here that the students are characterizing the robots on the basis of their own reactions to and interactions with the robots, not on the basis of what the robots intrinsically are. In other words, the students are using extrinsic features to characterize the robots, not intrinsic features. This difference parallels that between extrinsic human dignity and intrinsic human dignity that I discussed earlier.

Brooks, with whom I strongly disagree on almost all fronts, criticizes the idea that human beings are "special" in any important way and therefore deserve respect of a different kind. He believes that machines — including robots — will become more intelligent than us and therefore could deserve greater respect than we do. It merits noting that for Brooks, respect depends on intelligence — that is, on an "extrinsic performance" characteristic — not on being human, an "intrinsic worth" characteristic. When this approach is applied to humans, it attaches value to us according to what we do, not who we are — that is, human. If we accept this view, then humans are more accurately described as "human doings" than "human beings." It is clear that the developments in robotics and artificial intelligence will challenge our traditional concepts of what is a "being" and what is a "creature," and what kinds and degrees of respect are owed different life forms, especially humans. This discussion raises many questions, among them: What constitutes a being? What constitutes a creature? Is there a difference between beings and creatures? Do humans deserve respect as beings different from other beings and creatures? And if so, upon what is that respect predicated?

To turn to the last question first: I, like many people, believe that humans are special beings and therefore deserve special respect *simply because they are human*. This belief probably reflects my moral intuition to that effect. But is there any other way that we can justify seeing human beings, and respect for them, as special?

Let's look at the language we have traditionally used to describe ourselves and other life forms. We speak of creatures and beings. Is there a difference between them? The *Oxford English Dictionary* tells us that the word "being" is often used as shorthand for human being, while "creature" is used to distinguish other life forms from human beings. But merely differentiating other living entities from ourselves is not, in itself, a justification for a difference in respect. The word person is also often used as a synonym for human being. This term invokes the philosophical and legal concept of personhood, which is specific to humans and does carry a requirement of special respect. But again, on what basis are we justified in making that distinction?

Could we say that one important distinction is between *natural* beings or creatures and *artificially* created ones? That depends upon whether there is a difference in kind or just in degree between them, and as we have discussed, not everyone agrees about that. Perhaps the definition of "creature" holds answers. How extensive is that definition? Does it include entities we have constructed that are alive — for instance, new viruses artificially made through synthetic biology? Have we truly created this virus, or just constructed it from already existing materials? We certainly did not create the elements of the DNA and RNA that make up its genes.

On the other hand, when we turn our attention to the qualities of a being in order to decide whether robots, for instance, are beings, we must ask: Does a being have to be alive? If so, what are the criteria for being alive? We might answer that an entity has to be self-repairing, self-replicating, and self-sustaining in order to be alive. If so, nanobots might be alive. Or must a being also be conscious of its own existence? In that case, are amoebas, cats, or dogs beings? Not if we add the requirement that they must also have a sense of their own personal history to qualify as a being or person. In that case are deeply, permanently unconscious people beings? They are if we accept, as most — although not all — of us do, that present or past awareness of one's existence and history is a sufficient criterion for remaining a human being worthy of the respect that entails. But that excludes embryos and fetuses, which many of us believe deserve respect as human beings. All of this brings us back to the point at which we started: that special respect for human beings is, and should continue to be, predicated on nothing more than having human origins.

One way to express the belief and moral intuition that humans are special, and therefore deserve special respect, is through the concept of soul (for those who are religious in an Abrahamic tradition) or human spirit (for those who are not religious). And note that even religions such as Hinduism and Buddhism, which teach that animals have souls, regard humans as distinct from animals and deserving of special respect. In other words, the possession of soul or human spirit is the way we establish a difference in kind, not just in degree, between humans and other living entities (wonder-inspiring as they are), and therefore a difference in the kind of respect owed to each.

Even if we accept that robots are beings and that there is a difference in kind between "full flesh" beings (humans) and those that are fully machines (robots), and therefore a difference the respect owed to each, on which side of the human being/other being divide do part-machine part-human entities fall? Let us look at the xenotransplantation debate for insights here. Complement genes are species-specific genes that enable an animal's body to detect whether a transplanted organ comes from the same species as itself or from a different species. To avoid the hyper-acute rejection that would otherwise occur with a cross-species transplant — such as using pig organs in humans — human-complement genes are inserted in pig embryos that are intended as future organ donors. The body of the human recipient will then react as though the pig organ came from another human. Otherwise, it would reject the organ within the first hour after transplant. It is commonly accepted that the pig with those human complement genes is still a pig, if one that has human complement genes. The same is true when we put technological parts into a human — we still have a human but with technological parts. If, however, we design a technological creature with some human genes to activate it, this creature is actually a technological entity, not a human one. Let's look more closely at this assumption: What if the creature was comprised of fifty percent technology or machine and fifty percent human genes? Or what if the genes we transferred coded for human brain cells?

At the beginning of this chapter, I raised the question of a chimpanzee embryo in which we replace the two percent of genes that differ from those of a human embryo with the relevant human genes. Is a being with a ninety-eight percent chimpanzee genotype (its genes are ninety-eight percent chimpanzee) but a human phenotype (it looks like a human) chimp or human? Most of us have a strong moral intuition that there is that something deeply ethically troubling about crossing the species barrier — that is, in making chimeras, especially between humans and other animals. Indeed, the Canadian Assisted Human Reproduction Act prohibits creating a chimera with heavy criminal penalties. There is a loophole in the act, however — almost certainly an intentional one. While placing a cell of any non-human life form into a human embryo is prohibited, the converse is not. It is likely this loophole was allowed to facilitate the development of xenotransplantation, but it does open up other possibilities. Scientist Ian Wilmut, the creator of Dolly the sheep, the first animal cloned from an adult somatic cell, once said that such possibilities had never been anticipated by nature and therefore nature had not developed any protections against them. But if we belong to the "ethics camp" that believes that nothing is inherently wrong, why not make chimeras if great benefit could come from doing so?

Perhaps in discussing specific questions such as this we will be able to agree that doing some things is inherently wrong. Such issues bring us back to the concept of human dignity we discussed previously. If we see human dignity as intrinsic and unique to humans, then only humans have it because it is part of the essence of being human and is not part of the essence of any other being. This dignity is different in kind from any respect or dignity owed to other living beings or creatures. However, if we say that human dignity is extrinsic — that it is conferred on us because others see us as meriting dignity when we display certain qualities or characteristics, not just because we are human — then, depending upon what qualities we value, a sophisticated robot could (as some people propose) merit even more "human" dignity than some seriously disabled humans.

There are, of course, dangers in glorifying the natural (as I could be accused of doing in relation to humans), but valuing it can act as an important safeguard against redesigning human nature as the transhumanists urge us to do. Perhaps not one but two important features mark why humans deserve special respect: first, we are natural — not artificially created by other humans; and second, simply because we are human. But as we have seen, some people don't agree that there's anything intrinsically special about being human. And that disagreement is at the heart of our disagreements about the ethics of using the new technoscience to alter human nature.

Let's look at what qualities or attributes might make humans special. Currently, the fact that humans can discover knowledge and create sophisticated technologies is what distinguishes us from other animals and from robots. But it is possible that, in the future, robots may also be knowledge-discoverers. Indeed, they could be better at it than humans, if they were programmed as such. In that case, should we distinguish between biological and non-biological intelligence, or should we treat such robots as equally worthy as humans of respect and protection? But even if we assume that machines do "reason" and accept that the ability to reason is part of intelligence, I would strongly dispute that the ability to reason comprises the totality of human intelligence — such a belief comes from thinking that reason is the only important way of human knowing. Moreover, does the fact that we have created machines with the ability to reason mean that, as the creators, we are "superior" to the machines, or at least deserving of more respect? This raises an interesting possibility for those who believe in God — the possibility that God created us to find knowledge, just as we might create robots to do. (Indeed, there are some Christians who believe that God intended humans to discover the new molecular biology and genetic technologies in order to become co-creators with Him of future humans.)

Margaret Visser, in her Massey Lectures *Beyond Fate*, takes a different view. She sees the robot as monster, one that puts humanity on trial and questions our definition of ourselves, as monsters have always done.[6] Some disturbing possibilities and connections flow from that idea. For instance, just as we "give birth" to robots in designing and making them, through the use of new reproductive technologies we could in the future give birth to children we have designed and "made" ourselves. If, as Visser says, the robots we create are monsters, might the children we create through the use of technology be the same? And if robots are indeed monsters, and if we do not believe in the intrinsic dignity of humans, might we be creating non-human monsters that could eliminate us, if not physically then in the sense of being "superior" to us?[7]

As these issues and examples illustrate, the consequences of our technological resourcefulness are precisely what require our ethical resourcefulness. Technology can make us feel helpless, when (ironically) it is supposed to empower us. Thoughts and attitudes such as "we can't stop it," "if we don't allow it, other people will," "the horse is out of the barn," and the technological-imperative syndrome ("have technology, must use") display fatalism, nihilism, loss of control, loss of hope — in short, a moral bankruptcy that is a deeply worrying.

I believe we need an antidote to this loss of hope — a topic I discuss in greater depth in later. I also believe that hope depends on having a feeling of connection to the future — and even more than that, a future we believe we can affect for the "good." Perhaps believing that we can have a positive impact on the future is the essence of hope. This belief can generate the desire to leave a legacy, in that legacies have an impact on and affect the future. Many people die more peacefully when they can see they are leaving a legacy. On the other hand, if the future seems to be one we can't affect, we will believe there is no point in doing anything now — we might as well be passive and inactive. These are signs of major depression, the antithesis of hope. This is indeed how many people feel about technology — that there is nothing they can do to affect how it is used in the future. I believe that searching for a shared ethics to govern our use of technology is one way to overcome that feeling.

To return to the topic of the nature of robots, I propose that the difference between us and them is — dare I say it — our human spirit and soul (whatever we take the latter to mean). I wonder if the advent of highly intelligent robots might mean that investigations into the nature of human spirit and soul will become more important than in the recent past? Will we see reactions against both the "we are gene machines" ("genes R us") view and the "human" view of machines ("robots R us")? We humans initially expressed the distinction between ourselves and animals by saying that we are different in kind because humans have souls. Then, with the advent of some theories of evolution and concepts such as speciesism, some of us saw ourselves as simply the highest class of animals. Most recently, with the new genetic knowledge, others among us see humans as gene machines. With the further development of robotics and artificial intelligence, will these same people soon see themselves as machines (cyborgs, robots, human robots) and accept that we should take the necessary steps to become just that? The latter view is the one transhumanists want all of us to share — a post-human future in which people like us, whom the transhumanists call "unmodified (natural) humans," are obsolete models.

Convergence

Before we look in more detail at what transhumanists believe, let me define *convergence*. Convergence refers to the concurrent use of several technologies, which leads to results that are different in degree, and often in kind, from those that would be possible using each technology individually. Convergence is not a new phenomenon — atomic science and aeronautical engineering (aircraft technology) converged to make possible the dropping of the atomic bomb on Hiroshima.

The current hot topic in convergence, one that is central to this chapter, is the convergence of nanotechnology, biotechnology and biomedicine, information technology, and cognitive sciences (sometimes referred to as NBIC).[8] Some predict "the convergence of NBIC technologies will increase human potential at a speed that may eclipse the scientific and technological developments of the last millennium in a fraction of that time."[9] NBIC is of great interest to the pharmaceutical industry because of the potential for advanced diagnostics and therapies, and to the military because of the potential to develop armour that provides tactical awareness and cognition in "field activity." For example, the super-warriors of the future will receive signals to their brains from helmet-mounted cameras, sonar, and other equipment. A device known as a BrainPort provides a link between the soldiers' helmets and tongues, and from there, signals are passed to their brains. Scientists at the Florida Institute for Human and Machine Cognition have developed this device, with which they "hope to give elite soldiers superhuman senses similar to owls, snakes, and fish."[10] One day we may have to decide whether it is ethical to implant such devices in humans instead of in helmets — that is, whether it is ethical to create human techno-warriors.

In short, NBIC will raise many unprecedented ethical questions because, like many groundbreaking scientific developments, it has "near boundless potential for good" and also has potential for serious harm. Its development requires ethical and responsible stewardship at national and international levels. Our development and use of atomic energy, which continues to face us with humanity-threatening issues in both its peaceful and military uses, provides an important lesson from recent history in this regard.

The ethics of technological convergence go beyond the ethics of the immediate technology being developed. In developing a code of ethics, we must respond to difficult questions such as this one: How broadly must a person in one field consider the possible harmful outcome of convergence with another field in assessing the ethics of what they do?[11] Scientists, in particular, often object to being limited in what they do by the responses to these inquiries. The ethics of convergence must be an ethics of complexity — an ethics that accommodates substantial uncertainty about important factors because unknown risks are likely to be a major concern. I will discuss an ethics of complexity later.

Transhumanism

A new spectrum of terms started to appear on web sites shortly after the beginning of the new millennium. In 2003, I was introduced to the "human, transhuman, posthuman" continuum when I was asked by Simon Smith, the Toronto-based editor-in-chief of the transhumanist web site www.betterhumans.com, to debate American transhumanist James Hughes at a conference at the University of Toronto. I had never heard of transhumanism, and my first response was to think that one of my friends was playing a joke on me. But I went to Google and typed in transhumanism. To my surprise, 15,100 sites popped up — and as of August 2006, that number had risen to 1.8 million.

You probably know what humanism is: the American Humanists Association defines it as "a progressive philosophy of life that, without supernaturalism, affirms our ability and responsibility to lead ethical lives of personal fulfillment that lead to the greater good of humanity."[12] But you might not know what transhumanism or posthumanism is. In a nutshell, transhumanists believe that revolutions now occurring in info-, bio- nano-, robotic-, AI-(artificial intelligence) technologies will converge to alter the fundamental nature of being human, and with that our concepts of what it means to be human. We and all our most important values and beliefs will be changed beyond present recognition. Eventually, the transhumanists propose, we will reach the nirvana of a posthuman future: we won't be human at all.

The term *posthumanist* is interesting in that it includes the prefix *post*. If we look at how that prefix is commonly used — postmodernism, postfeminism, post-antibiotic, postsecular — we can see that we are saying we know what we were, and we know we are no longer that, but we don't yet know what we have become.

Transhumanists are enthusiastic supporters of NBIC convergence. The transhumanist vision is that through technology humans can and ought to become post-humans. For them, "human" is not the end of evolution; it is the beginning. They are techno-utopians and, like all utopians, they want more. This statement is not intended as a put-down of utopians or transhumanists. There's nothing wrong with dreaming about a better society — indeed, we all need to do so. Technoscience provides transhumanists with a strong negative answer to the existential question most of us ask ourselves at some point, Is this all there is? Transhumanism is not just a new concept; more accurately, it is a new world view, or perhaps even a secular religion. I have spoken previously about our longing for transcendence and its link to transformation.

For the transhumanists, the power of technoscience allows a new form of transcendence and transformation: going beyond and transforming ourselves by becoming posthuman. We can see transhumanism as an expression of the longing for transcendence and, through that, transformation. Transhumanists seek this experience and outcome through science, and we must therefore acknowledge a link between science, transcendence, and transformation just as there is a link between religion, transcendence, and transformation. In this respect, science and religion are playing the same role and facilitating the same human experience. One might even say that sometimes science functions as a "religion."

Transhumanists want to do good: They "seek to expand technological opportunities for humans to live longer and healthier lives and to enhance their intellectual, physical, psychological and emotional capacities."[13] At face value, most of us would endorse those goals. But the overall and ultimate goal of transhumanism is articulated more fully in the definition of a posthuman: "A person of unprecedented physical, intellectual, and psychological capacity; a self-programming, self-constituting, potentially immortal individual; a person who no longer can be classified usefully with Homo sapiens as the result of fundamental and sweeping modifications to inherited genetics, physiology, neurophysiology and neurochemistry." A posthuman future, then, is a future in which humans as we know them will have become obsolete and will be replaced by superior beings created by redesigning Homo sapiens with technoscience such as genetics, artificial intelligence technology, robotics, and nanotechnology (atomtech). We will become *Techno sapiens*.

Whether or not we agree with the goals and philosophy of the transhumanists, they are doing us a major service in making us aware of the enormity of the techno-cultural transformation the new technoscience could effect. They see the future development of human nature itself as no longer being "limited to traditional humanistic methods, such as education and cultural development." Rather, transhumanists believe we can "use technology to move beyond what some think of as 'human'" to discover and create our authentic (technological) selves.

I have argued elsewhere that we contemporary humans are uncomfortable with — even frightened by — mystery, and that our response to our fear is to convert mysteries into problems with technological solutions. For example, euthanasia — a lethal injection — is a technological response to the mystery of death after it has been converted to the problem of death.[14] Might transhumanism be a similar response to the mystery of life? It converts the mystery of life into the problem of life, and seeks technological solutions to that problem. But could it prove to be a lethal injection to the human spirit — our deepest sense of what it means to be human and ability to find meaning in life?

Practical Realities: Steps Toward Transhumanism

Transhumanists argue that we should not be frightened of their world view because we have already accepted and taken steps toward it. As I will explain, although it is dangerous to agree with that argument, it is nonetheless true that we have already made incremental and subtle changes in our understanding of humanness that can be characterized as steps toward a posthuman future — for instance, changes in how we perceive human identity. We used to see ourselves as integrally whole from birth to death — at most, missing a few parts from accidents or surgery. With transplants, we accepted a modular theory of human identity: "Interchangeable Parts R Us." In the future, these interchangeable parts could become enhancement technologies — genetic modification or computer chips implanted in our brains.

Our perceptions of our bodies have also changed as a result of technology — for example, older people see cell-phones as pieces of technology to be used; younger people see them as extensions of their ears. Physical enhancement of our bodies through cosmetic surgery and psychological modification through mood-altering drugs are now regarded as routine, normal, and beneficial — at least until recent disclosures about the dangers of these drugs, especially that of suicide. The transhumanists argue what they envision is just the next step along this same path, and therefore that vastly more invasive and radical technologies, such as dramatically enhancing human intelligence, are already ethically valid because they are no different in kind from those we have already accepted.

Seeing technology as part of ourselves, rather than as something separate from us that we use, can have wide-ranging and unexpected effects. For example, how we see our bodies can affect how we define euthanasia. When we turn the natural person into the technological person, we blur the lines between natural death, "technological death," and euthanasia. If we see technology as a part of ourselves, and if removing it causes us to die, we can see that removal as an intervention that kills us. The person (defined in this case as including technology) dies from — is killed by — the technology's removal. It can then be argued that this removal of technology is euthanasia, and if we agree with euthanasia in that form, to be consistent we should agree with it in any form, including through lethal injection. If, however, we see the technology as foreign — not as part of the essential person — removing it is not intervening on the person to kill them; rather, its removal allows the natural person to die naturally. That is the antithesis of euthanasia.

Aging

As described by the transhumanists, the benefits promised by the new technologies are deeply seductive; transhumanists make the sirens of old look like amateurs, especially when they neglect to emphasize the risks of using technoscience.[15] Transhumanists are great optimists; they turn on its head the old warning that the man who strives to be a god is doomed. Instead, transhumanists believe that physical immortality through technoscience (they refer to this as man becoming a god) is an option that will be open to posthumans.

It is no accident that the issues of life-prolongation and age-retardation are front and centre on the pro-technology agenda. The transhumanists, probably rightly, believe these issues will appeal to many people, and in doing so will generate support for transhumanism and posthumanism. If, as we will be sorely tempted to do, we accept radical life extension, then why not cloning, designing our children, reproducing entirely artificially, enhancing our intelligence with computer chip implants, becoming cyborgs, and eventually being superseded by robots that are infinitely more intelligent and durable than we are?[16]

Life-prolongation involves using technology to extend our "natural" life spans by repairing or replacing our "parts" as they wear out. At conferences to discuss the social, ethical, and economic implications of transhumanism, scholars have pegged the "new normal" life span with life-prolongation at 125 to 150 years. The implications of this are staggering: for instance, at any given time humans have always had one generation in charge, one growing up, and one aging and dying. Life prolongation would give us up to four concurrent generations capable of being in charge. We have no experience with such a situation, and our institutions are not designed to accommodate it.

The implications of age retardation are far more radical. The technology involves reprogramming, at the embryonic stage, the genes that control aging so that we would reach puberty around forty years of age, early middle age at eighty years, and old age much later, if ever. The advocates of this technology speak seriously of ultimate immortality. The changes and problems we would face are completely unprecedented.

Our relationship to our bodies has changed with the advent of the new technoscience, which allows us to vastly augment the search for eternal youth. But that search affects much more than our physical selves. It also affects our emotional, intuitive, psychological, and spiritual selves. For instance, to return here to the topic I explored earlier, that of our connection to nature, I believe that experiencing this deep connection, and thereby feeling profound respect for nature, may be a feature of aging. This may be why old people have traditionally been revered for their wisdom and have had the privilege and obligation to protect and hand down that wisdom to younger generations. We now know that animals — and in all likelihood, humans — have genes that must be activated (imprinted) during a critical period when they are young, failing which the genes shut down permanently. Might we also have genes that cannot be activated before a certain relatively advanced age, genes that allow us to experience realities that result in wisdom?

I have often mused that some normal loss of memory as one ages might allow older people to see the big picture — the forest — while younger people are still looking at individual matters — the trees — as they need to and should do. Indeed, recent neurological research shows that young people are better at mental tasks that require precise perception while older people are better at those tasks that require a comprehensive overall view.[17] Perhaps this might be a manifestation of a group survival mechanism, one that allows a society to have a range of skills at its disposal, especially for input into critical decision-making.

How might the current bias toward being forever young, no matter what one's chronological age, affect our societies? Might it be that becoming more conservative as we age is a safety net for society that allows the young to try out radical approaches to collective values, without doing serious harm to those values? Without that safety net, harm is much more likely. Indeed, the safety net is of unprecedented importance in deciding the values that should govern the new science.

But aging is not for sissies or cowards. In the Czech movie *Autumn/Spring*, one old man says to another old man, his lifetime friend, "Our paths have nowhere to go." These men still have paths, but they go nowhere; to compensate, they set up a "game" of pretending to own expensive mansions that they purport to sell to wealthy people — in short, a fraud scheme. But they do this only to amuse themselves, not to make money from those they mislead. Many old people probably just give up entirely, and this is destructive to them and society in many ways — not least because, as I have pointed out previously, maintaining hope requires a sense of connection to the future. Without a path into the future, that connection is lost. When as a society we saw elders as fonts of wisdom, the paths of elderly people went somewhere. That somewhere was a contribution to both the present and the future — it was a legacy. Old people were valued, respected, helped others, and could experience hope to the end of their lives. Today, many old people, who could still contribute and be fulfilled in doing so, fill their days with personally meaningless, societally useless activities.

This is not their fault; society makes it difficult for them to do otherwise. But our treatment of our elders is the ultimate example of the results of our society's intense individualism and hedonism, with a sad and tragic edge. The intense individualism so often translates into intense loneliness, and the hedonism is destructive and undesirable.

Elderly people who are able to remain curious about life, God, art, and the world, and who believe they are making a contribution, have much to teach us. My eighty-five-year-old aunt, Veronica, and her ninety-year-old boyfriend, Neil, are powerful examples. Both are sought out by many people for assistance and advice, which they provide with a healthy dose of optimism and realism — Veronica was formerly matron of a hospital, where she supported her patients in their joys and sorrows. She used to do early-morning rounds as the night staff signed off and the day staff signed on. One morning she was standing by the bed of a patient who had had his leg amputated the previous day. She spoke with him for awhile, and as she was leaving she turned and said, "You'll be fine, Captain Long John Silver" (a reference to the one-legged pirate in Robert Louis Stevenson's book *Treasure Island*). Patient and matron both burst out laughing. Recently, Neil was seriously ill and in intensive care, but against all the odds he survived. I sympathized with Veronica about the loss of the social life she had with Neil and the fatigue of trekking to the hospital (she doesn't drive a car and insists on using public transport). She replied, "We like to see each other, and although we miss the fun of the events we went to and the people we saw, it's just the same in a different setting."

Throughout our lives we all need someone to love, something to do, and something to hope for. So often, old people are denied all three. Tragically, we can speak of an epidemic of loneliness among older people in the developed world. Human ethics — if not human rights — demands that all of us, as individuals, communities, and a society, make it otherwise.

Neuroethics

The new science means that not only can we redesign our bodies, but we can also redesign our minds. Probably no other possibility for redesigning ourselves raises such serious ethical questions. Advances in the neurosciences are so major and raise such profound issues, including ethical ones, that the first hundred years of the new millennium have been proclaimed the Century of the Brain. Neuroscientists are seeking to solve the puzzle of human consciousness and unravel the secrets of an organ described as the most complex in the universe. Earlier, I spoke about the ethics of designing our children by genetically altering them when they are embryos. I explained how Jürgen Habermas argues that doing so is unethical because it means these children are not free. They are deprived of the liberty that comes from the fact that no one has interfered with the essence of one's being and that, as a result, one's genetic makeup has come into existence through chance. Moreover, because these children are not equal to the designer, they are deprived of equality. I also proposed that those losses of liberty and equality have implications far beyond the persons directly affected. For instance, because the liberty and equality of all citizens is at the heart of democracy, to create people who are neither free nor equal undermines the basis of democracy.

As profoundly worrying as is any such intervention on a person's physical characteristics, our level of concern is exponentially augmented when the intervention is to design a person's psyche — permanently, through surgery or genetic manipulation, or (much less concerning but still worrisome) temporarily through psychopharmacological agents. Possibilities that have been discussed in the literature include creating fearless, pain-free soldiers and designing less-intelligent humans to do the jobs "genetically rich" (genetically intellectually enhanced) humans won't want to do. What would this mean to the differences between us that make us unique as human beings? To the concept of free will and responsibility for one's actions that flow from that? To the concepts of criminal law and criminal responsibility? To our sense of morality? To our ideas of what constitutes merit?

We live in a therapeutic culture where normal human functioning is medicalized, often to promote treatments for the illnesses created through that medicalization. For instance, shyness becomes "social phobia disorder," which can be treated with an expensive drug. I'm not denying that some people have mental illnesses and benefit greatly from treatment. But when all human sadness becomes depression and the number of people diagnosed with depression and sales of antidepressants soar, or when shy people are labelled as having social phobia disorder and prescribed drugs, or when a large percentage of young boys are given drug treatment for attention deficit hyperactivity disorder, or when normal sleepiness is characterized as a new illness when a drug to prevent sleepiness becomes available, we must seriously question our assumptions and actions.

Advances in the neurosciences challenge not only our physical functioning but also our culture. A promotional brochure for a recent conference on "The Neurosciences and Contemporary Society" puts it this way: "A Century of the Brain . . . signals the omnipresence of the brain as a major icon of contemporary culture — from literature and the plastic arts, to medical ethics, to theology and religion, to emerging research areas such as neuroeconomics or neuroeducation, and to an expanding galaxy of more or less extravagant neurobeliefs and neuropractices. The conference intends to explore various aspects of the history, sociology, anthropology, and presence and consequences of the cerebral subject as a major figure of contemporary culture."[18]

Perhaps the greatest danger opened up by advances in cognitive science is that our extraordinary new knowledge about the human brain and mind might lead to reductionism about what it means to be human — a loss of appreciation of the ineffable, numinous qualities of the human mind and spirit. David Rothenberg, a philosopher of music, suggests an approach that could help prevent that. Rothenberg refers to neuropsychologist Steven

Pinker's "'auditory cheesecake' hypothesis, which states that music is essentially useless as an adaptive force in natural selection."[19] Rather, it's like cheesecake — a momentary pleasure with no larger purpose or outcome. Rothenberg responds: "If the theory of natural selection can't explain music, there may be something wrong with the theory, not the song. . . . The mainstream of evolutionary theory is not so easily able to account for the blues, for jazz, for heavy metal or the classical symphony. Nor can it explain the vast diversity and complexity of bird songs, which are sung much more than a functionalist view of birds mating and fighting would allow. There's too much complexity, too much joy, too much at stake in the music itself. 'The bird sings because it has a song.' Only birds, whales, and humans are able to learn to make different sounds than those they are born with. . . . [C]ognitive science has something to learn from music, the human art that so touches us in feelings nearly impossible to describe." Rothenberg warns us about being "too willing at the end to succumb to the rationalizing dogmas of cognitive science, rather than remind[ing ourselves] . . . how the most beautiful aspects of our lives often elude explanation."[20]

The Search for Perfection, and Disabled People

One of the most important questions we must ask ourselves about using the new technoscience to redesign ourselves and our descendants is what impact our enhanced ability to search for perfection in ourselves, our children, and others — and to eliminate those we see as imperfect — will have on disabled people and societal values?

"Positive eugenics" is the use of genetic technologies to enhance the people on whom they are used. "Negative eugenics" is the elimination of those who are seen as genetically inferior. In the practice of negative eugenics, disabled people become disposable people. The Nazi horrors showed us the dangers of a political platform or public policy approach that uses science and technology to search for perceived biological "perfection" in ourselves and society. That approach is based purely on reason, unmodified by other ways of human knowing — for instance, by human memory, examined emotions, moral intuition — and untouched by the important knowledge we receive from the "messy human soul."

Recently, a friend of mine wept as she told me how the members of her immediate and extended family are traumatized and grieving because her son and his wife, who was twenty-plus weeks pregnant, decided after much agonizing discussion in which all members of the extended family were involved, that it was better to have an abortion than give birth to a child with spina bifida. What would it mean, to eliminate most people with this condition from our society? Earlier I asked what other categories of people will be eliminated — the profoundly deaf, those with bipolar disorder (manic-depressive illness), or those with achondroplasia (short-statured people)? And who decides which people to eliminate? At present, it is either the pregnant woman or the woman and the child's father if the woman wants to involve him.

Some parents are aborting fetuses with a cleft palate — a relatively minor problem that can be treated with surgery — at thirty-two weeks' gestation. It is difficult to argue they should not be allowed to do so when, as is true in Canada, there are no legal restrictions on abortion or prohibition of it at any stage of pregnancy and "absolute rights of reproductive freedom" are promoted as the norm. The use of these technologies is often informed only by intense individualism — that is, allowing individuals' personal preferences to rule, without due consideration of the risks and harms to society and its values that doing so might entail. Even people who are pro-choice need to take such risks and harms into account if they are to make decisions that are ethical.

Quite apart from the question of whether at least some abortions — such as those that involve viable fetuses — should be considered inherently wrong, we need to ask what impact such decisions, especially when they become widespread as they are now doing, will have on people with disabilities and their feelings of self-worth, of being valued by others and society? And what will society lose in allowing the elimination of these people? I believe we will lose the lessons in courage, hope, perseverance, balance, and acceptance, to name just a few that these people bring as a unique gift to us. And we are highly likely to reduce our capacity to be humble, and diminish our own empathy, compassion, acceptance of difference, and respect for all human lives. I believe that our moral intuition in these situations often tells us there is something wrong, or at least very worrying, about our decisions, but we suppress that intuition with "pure" or technical reason — the person is better off not existing, we can have another child, and so on. We must always question whether these decisions are fundamentally self-serving — narcissistic and egocentric — although cloaked in a rationale that allows us to avoid causing another person to suffer.

We have tried to avoid labelling our decisions to eliminate disabled people (indeed, we usually speak only of eliminating disability, which is telling) as eugenic by suggesting that such decisions belong only to individuals and are purely personal, and by medicalizing the decisions. However, putting on the cloak of medicine often dulls our moral intuitions and makes us oblivious to the ethical dangers of what we are doing. Medicalizing an issue is not neutral; rather, in the case of "avoiding disability" — avoiding disabled people — it often involves making eugenic decisions that can have a profound impact on society. Most disabled adults tell us that they would not have wanted to be aborted, so why do we assume that aborting them is justified on medical grounds? As Alice Domurat Dreger says, in writing about separating conjoined twins even when one will die, "How much is this about our view of the discrete individual as normal, how much about the needs of the person(s) themselves? It raises interesting questions about the manner in which social and cultural [aspects] are transposed to medical [ones]."[21] When combined with the new technoscience, the search for perfection in ourselves, our children, our pets, our death — "the perfect death" through euthanasia and assisted suicide — is fraught with ethical dangers, and nowhere more so than when we believe perfection lies in going beyond being human.

Ensuring We "First Do No Harm"

So what do we need to do to ensure that these amazing new powers placed in our hands by science are not used unethically (that we first do no harm) and are used ethically (where possible we do good), especially in maintaining our humanness and humaneness? Answering that question requires us to look again at some of the concepts we have explored in previous chapters — concepts such as a shared ethics, the secular sacred, and a presumption in favour of the natural.

As well, I want to look further at a particular aspect of the idea of a shared ethics — namely, the role that the much disputed concept of truth might play. I pointed out earlier the danger of seeking "the Truth" as a way to find a shared ethics. Nonetheless, I do believe we need to search for some form of truth to ground a shared ethics that will protect the integrity of the human race and individual people as we explore the possibilities of the new technoscience. Simplistic — even trite — as it might sound, I propose that our best chance of finding a shared ethics is to search for what we see as our true, ethical human selves, whether physically, intellectually, emotionally, or spiritually, as individuals, communities, and societies. In the past, because we couldn't change what "human" meant, we had no need to articulate what constituted it exactly. That is no longer true, as we have seen. If we are to respond convincingly to propositions that we should change human nature, such as those the trans-humanists are putting forward, we must understand what is valuable in that nature and decide what must be preserved at all costs. The word that comes to mind is *authenticity* — what is authentic in human nature, its very essence, without which that essence is lost?

I recently had an exchange of ideas with a colleague, Daniel Levitin, who is a professor of psychology and music at McGill University and interested in comparing the experiences of people listening to music virtually to those listening to a live performance. His investigation caused me to wonder why seeing the original of a famous painting is not only different from, but much more excit-ing than, seeing an exact copy — at least, to me it is. (It turns out that some people prefer the copy. For instance, the Australian government built a replica of part of the Great Barrier Reef to reduce the number of tourists to the real reef in order to better protect it. Tourists from Japan preferred the replica to the real thing.) Or we can think about how antiques lose their value if they are refinished — when the many human hands that have touched the antique have been erased, we consider that the antique is no longer authentic, that its priceless intangible essence is gone. In fact, we value such antiques less because in our touching them to alter them, they can no longer touch our imagination with the same profundity. I believe that if the transhumanists achieve their goals, we will have lost our authenticity, our human essence, our messy, old, much-touched soul. We will be like refinished antiques: no longer unique, no longer the "real thing."

Toward Finding our True, Ethical, Human Selves Through a Shared Ethics

Whether we frame our quest for a shared ethics as a search for truth or as a search for our true ethical human selves might not matter in terms of results, but the latter is likely to appeal to many more people than the former. Still, no matter how we frame our quest, we must decide what we understand by "truth" in the context of a shared ethics. For instance, to say either that God does or does not exist is not "true," in the sense that such statements can neither be proved nor disproved scientifically. Nor can we all agree on one position or the other as a fact. Therefore, neither view can define for all of us what we mean by our true, ethical human selves nor found the shared base on which we can establish values we hold in common. If we are going to find a shared ethical base, that base must be able to accommodate both those who believe in God and those who do not — in short, it must not be antithetical to either. This requires that we translate our values, whatever their base, into a language we can all share. Earlier, I discussed the importance of our choice of language in both searching for a shared ethics and doing ethics. Here I merely want to emphasize that religious people must try to speak their truth in secular language, and non-religious people must avoid speaking their truth in anti-religious language, if we are to engage in constructive dialogue.

It merits pointing out here that both those who are certain God does not exist and those who are certain that He does make finding a shared ethics difficult when they seek to impose their respective beliefs on others. Often, the opposing views of these two groups are styled as a conflict between science and religion, and as a consequence the groups are seen as radically different from each other. But there are important similarities. Both have faith — one group, that science shows them God does not exist; the other, that religion shows them that He does — and both are certain they are right (and the other group, wrong).

In dealing with this, we must keep in mind the following: First, that faith and doubt, whether in relation to science or religion, are not opposites. Rather, doubt is the shadow side of faith, and certainty is the opposite of both. But accepting uncertainty requires humility and the courage to live with it. Second, we can distinguish between what we know through science and what can only be known in other ways, and between the unknown and the unknowable on the one hand, and nothingness on the other. Many people on the science side of the science-versus-religion debate assume that what we can't know through science does not exist — they equate that which is unknown or unknowable through science with non-existence. This is a mistake. While science can tell us what is not true within the realm it explores through falsifiable hypotheses, even in that realm (let alone any other one) it cannot tell us *all* that is true. For instance, science can affirm through observation that not all bears are white; but even if scientists had only ever seen white bears they could never affirm that all bears are white, only that they had not discovered one.

The common ground between those who take a principle-based approach to ethics (many of whom found their principles in religious or spiritual beliefs) and many, but not all, of those who are moral relativists[22] is that both believe they know and are promoting the truth — or at least a partial truth. Their polarization results from the opposite content of what they believe that truth to be. As I have explained previously, people who take a principle-based approach believe that we can say that some things are inherently wrong, and therefore we must not do those things no matter how much good could result. That is part of their truth. In contrast, utilitarians, including moral relativists, believe that the morality of any particular conduct is determined by the balance of good and harm it involves. This is part of their truth. The range of knowledge that is taken into account in the two approaches to "doing ethics" also differs radically. Because metaphysical beliefs cannot be objectively proven (they are beliefs, not provable facts) and ways of knowing such as long-standing, widely shared moral intuitions are not "hard science," these beliefs and ways of knowing are dismissed by relativists, who rely only on provable facts found through "pure" or technical reason. The resulting conflict can never be resolved — but again, it has to be accommodated.

How do we get around this tension? I suggest that we search for and focus on broadly shared moral intuitions and long-time, widely shared aspirations and ideas of "the good" in human life — intuitions and aspirations on which we can all agree although the reasons for our agreement might differ markedly. What we find through that combination I would call the truths of the "human spirit." In particular, I propose we need to search for the truths of the human spirit to guide us in making decisions about the unprecedented powers the new technoscience has given us over life itself, and over each individual life, so that those decisions will respect life and, in particular, the essence of our human nature — those elements without which we would no longer be human. That leads me back to nature and the natural, especially the nature of human nature.

Earlier, I explored the idea of using a presumption in favour of the natural as a procedural mechanism that could help us to draw lines between what is ethical and what is not when we exercise the powers the new science gives us. Here, I want to look briefly at what respect for the natural requires of us as we intervene on humans and the essence of human nature. Are there truths in human nature and the natural — the truths of the human spirit — that can help us to ethically use the new technoscience in intervening on ourselves?

I wrote previously about the wrongs of "designer embryos" and the "designer children" that result from them. I want to propose that it is not only individuals who need protection against being designed, but humankind itself. This is what the transhumanists' dreams show us. To ensure that the human race is not genetically altered, we must have a shared morality to protect us against such alteration. In other words, a shared morality is necessary if we are to remain human as we presently understand the meaning of that state. In particular, we need a morality to protect the human spirit — especially whatever genetic substrate this might possibly have.

Lately I have been pondering what insights we might find if we were to imagine ourselves as living in an encompassing human spirit (or soul) that holds all of us — perhaps, something akin to Carl Jung's "collective unconscious" — rather than seeing ourselves as each having an individual human spirit. This thought is part of my long-time musing that life owns us rather than the other way around. Might that encompassing spirit be what we call God, the Life Force, the Mystery of the Unknown, or whatever other term we choose to use? And in searching for ethics, are we searching to know how best to bring our conduct into line with that encompassing spirit?

Ultimately, we face a crucial question, one that in our multicultural, pluralistic, secular societies can no longer be answered by a shared religion: Why should we be moral at all? The short answer is this: because otherwise we would have a world that the vast majority of us would not want to live in.

As I was correcting a draft of this chapter, I was flying from Montreal to Beijing over the High Artic. I looked out the window of the airplane and thought, What a beautiful and amazing world! Please, don't let us mess it up! Our natural world includes us humans, and arguably the most important aspect of our world not to "mess up" is our very own nature. The new technoscience gives us the power to do that, and we are the first humans to have such a power. We must recognize that if we fail to use the new technoscience wisely and ethically, we could indeed "mess up" our world and ourselves. Ethics is fundamentally about not "messing it up" — not only for ourselves, but especially for future generations. I believe our primary obligation is not only to leave future generations with as many options — natural, material, ethical, spiritual — as we have, but, even more important, to leave them with nothing less than themselves — the miraculous outcome of 850 million years of evolution that, it is to be hoped, will also result in their children and their children's children in the generations to come.

V

PAST VIRTUES FOR A FUTURE WORLD:

HOLDING OUR HUMANNESS ON TRUST

"We need justice. We need toleration, honesty and moral courage. These are modern virtues without which we cannot hope to control the forces science has let loose among us."
— I. A. R. Wylie (1885–1959)

IN THIS LAST chapter, I want to explore the question of where we might go from here in searching for ethics, whether as individuals, families, communities, societies, or a global world. If we think back to the metaphor I used at the beginning of this book of a constellation of stars, what concepts, attributes, or capacities might we now want to find in that ethical constellation? Some that come to my mind are respect for nature, a sense of the sacred, the intellectual joy of reason, hope, awe, wonder, mystery, curiosity, creativity, intuition, trust, love, honesty, courage, integrity, compassion, kindness, generosity, restraint, and, I would add, a sense of humour. These are not all of the same nature or of equal importance, but all have roles to play in helping us to find meaning in life — which means they all have roles to play in helping us to find ethics.

Complexity

I want to begin, however, by looking at a concept that is relevant to all of the virtues, that of complexity — especially its relation to uncertainty and meaning-making.

The *Oxford English Dictionary* defines complexity as, "Involved nature or structure, intricacy. . . . A whole comprehending in its compass a number of parts, esp. (in later use) of interconnected parts or involved particulars; a complex or complicated whole." I suggest that complexity and meaning-making have a symbiotic relation: complexity is necessary for meaning-making, and meaning-making is necessary to deal with complexity. I've come to that conclusion through long-time puzzling about what ethicist David Roy meant when he said, "Suffering is where meaning crosses paths with biology." This seemed to me an important statement, but the more I thought about it the less I understood it — that is, until I looked at it in the light of complexity. Suffering cannot be accommodated in our lives, or even partially understood, unless we see it as an immensely complex phenomenon. When we, as biological creatures, witness suffering or suffer ourselves, and see this experience as complex, we have an opportunity to find meaning in life. It is not an opportunity the vast majority of us would seek — indeed, usually we do all we can to avoid it — but that does not take away from the great value many people find in suffering. Moreover, meanings are not always comforting and peaceful, and even when meanings *are* comforting they can be related to distressing ones. Roy relates how a patient describes the complex reality of finding meaning in suffering as experiencing the "sound of the soul singing, as it used to do before it lost its courage and its love." In short, finding true, complex meaning requires both courage and love.

There is a vast difference between simple and simplistic approaches to complex realities such as suffering and finding meaning. The former are valid and the latter are not. And when the simple is not sufficient, we need to tease out the elements that give rise to complexity if we are to deal with reality appropriately. My former law student Alicen Chen describes the complexity of a legal and ethical analysis of an issue this way: "An investigation that is textured, nuanced, layered and rich with traces of different cultures, disciplines, world views, and understandings of both human nature and human as compared to nature."

To reach a complex understanding of an issue, we might need to consider notions of objective and subjective; the knowable and the unknowable; the individual and the collective; duties to act and obligations to exercise restraint. We can undertake an analysis within these tensions, in the spaces between and among them, for it is there that room exists for complex understanding. Note, however, that we choose what we see as opposing forces in these tensions, and our choices are not neutral. They result from our values. We also generate creative tension when we simultaneously seek a single or individual principle or good and a universal one, especially when these cannot be reconciled and we choose to live with that situation. This discussion leads us to the insight that we should try to establish "creative tension" when that is called for.

In the same vein, let us consider the differences between thick and thin borders. The former have substantial overlap — they are fuzzy — while the latter provide clear dividing lines. Thick borders allow for the intermingling of concepts, ideas, and beliefs, which results in new insights and often a consensus that otherwise would be unavailable. People wander into one another's territory — into intellectual and ideological "no man's land" — still feeling that they are "at home." In doing so, they find what they have in common. Moreover, borders are always margins — for example, of academic disciplines — where creativity is more likely to occur. We can see this in most of the emerging scientific disciplines. So we should choose to work at the borders if we want to be creative in finding a shared ethics that can accommodate complexity — which, because of the very nature of a shared ethics, it must do.

Health-care management theorists Paul Plsek and Tim Wilson propose a way to work at the margins and thereby encourage creativity and its benefits.[1] They are looking at management and leadership, but their proposal applies equally to other contexts. They argue that we need to base our approach to issues on *complexity thinking*. This requires what they call a "minimum specifications" rule: give few specifics; describe boundaries, resources, permissions; and provide little overall direction. Loosening the boundaries in this way allows innovation. Complexity thinking applied to ethics shows that we can have a simple ethics methodology to govern complex ethics situations.

This raises the question: What does an ethics of complexity mean? Is it meant to govern complex situations, or to be a complex ethics, or both? Perhaps the most important point to make about complexity is that we need to identify it, whether it is factual or ethical or both, and deal with it accordingly. Complexity requires being comfortable with ambiguities, ironies and contradictions — in short, being comfortable with uncertainty. Dealing ethically with complexity and being comfortable with uncertainty are linked. We make ethical mistakes when we try to reduce necessary complexity to simplicity or necessary uncertainty to certainty. The result is approaches to ethics that are simple, certain, and wrong. These errors are made on both sides of the ethical divide.

Recognizing the difference between *uncertainty* and *indeterminacy* can also be important. Although the two words are often used as synonyms, even by the *Oxford English Dictionary*, and in this book I use uncertainty to indicate both, I want to distinguish between them here in order to point out a difference that can be important, including ethically. We sometimes need to distinguish between that which can be but is not at present known (that is, uncertainty) from that which cannot be known with certainty (that is, indeterminacy). In other words, uncertainty can be resolved by data when that data becomes available, but indeterminacy cannot. We may have to live with uncertainty (in either form) when we can't reconcile competing claims that seem equally meritorious — for example, with respect to access to limited health-care resources. Some people view themselves as "managing" uncertainty, but that often translates to obfuscation. The alternative is to openly accommodate it. That is more likely to avoid obfuscation — something that is often important ethically. We should keep in mind that we are much more likely to make ethical mistakes when we try to reconcile the irreconcilable instead of living with that which is irreconcilable and acknowledging what we are doing.

That brings to mind Isaiah Berlin's notion of "value pluralism."[2] In developing a theory of the moral order, Berlin postulates that values can be both true and irreconcilable at the same time, and that often societies are forced to choose between two competing goods rather than good and evil. For instance, for many Americans upholding the right to bear arms when there is an epidemic of deaths from small arms in America raises such an issue. In cases of this kind, there is a tension, and often an outright conflict, between respecting an individual's rights to self-determination and liberty, and protection of the community. Consequently, we are forced to choose which of these values we will honour and which we will breach. The same kind of conflict occurs when we breach people's rights to liberty by quarantining them to prevent the spread of SARS or Avian flu, or breach their rights to privacy in order to combat terrorism.

We need imagination to deal with complexity — in particular, imagination as exhibited in myth — not just reason. Our primary focus on reason may have deprived us of the ability to deal with complexity — for example, the complexities with which death faces us. Euthanasia is often presented as a reasoned response to death although a broad range of powerful emotions is usually in play. An extreme example of this is two pro-euthanasia physicians who have advocated the use of veterinarians and veterinary medicine as the best way to implement euthanasia; they argue that theirs is a totally rational, reasoned proposal. It can be compared (negatively, I believe) with imaginative responses to death, including those found in various religions. An important function of religion has been to keep us from adopting simplistic (simple but wrong) responses to complex realities such as death, and one way it did so was by keeping open ways of knowing in addition to reason.

Has our fear of uncertainty caused us to seek unitary ends (non-complex outcomes)? If so, have we lost a necessary balance — for instance, between respect for individual rights and fulfilling the needs of society? Seeking balance is a continuing process, not a once-and-forever outcome, and seeking balance and uncertainty are related. Often, we can seek balance only indirectly, and that requires us to live with uncertainty — that is, with the possibility of losing our balance. Again, we can ask what role religion has played in allowing people to live with uncertainty and to find balance in dealing with ethical complexity. It is important to note that not all religions can fulfill that role. It's a feature of fundamentalist religions, and fundamentalism in general (such as atheism and scientism) that its practitioners are certain they are correct. Consequently, they do not seek balance. I also note again that there is a substantive difference between balance and compromise, although sometimes the latter may be required to achieve the former.

Yet another danger that merits noting is confusing respect for methodology with respect for thought (or moral intuition, or imagination). Bureaucrats replace respect for thought or other ways of knowing with respect for methodology. Often, they do so to avoid dealing with complexity, either because it seems too difficult to deal with or because doing so is seen as politically risky. Politicians and bureaucrats will also try to avoid a socially complex issue, such as abortion, or same-sex marriage, or euthanasia, by handing it to the courts to deal with. Dealing with complexity requires humility — we must be able to say we don't know when that is the case. Bureaucrats — and their political masters — have great difficulty admitting that they don't know, especially when they fear that saying so is likely, as one politician put it, "to panic the public." The result is that bureaucrats and politicians — and others who do this — lose a sense of ethics.

Philosopher Charles Taylor is always worth quoting and that holds true in discussing complexity.[3] He says we have seen a victory of the mind and the will over complexity and spirit, and we have seen a victory of technology over mystery. In other words, we have lost complexity, spirit, and mystery, and replaced them with mind, will, and technology. The problem is not that the latter are bad or worthless; it's that they are necessary but not sufficient to living a fully human life. That is, they have replaced rather than supplemented the other features we need. Taylor's thinking also indicates that if we want to regain spirit and mystery, we must embrace complexity. Taylor points out that in our technological world, there are invisible processes (rather than people) that run our lives — for example, capitalism's drive for profit and our development of technology for this purpose. Moreover, since no one person or group of people runs the market, we do not know what impact the technology we develop will have on the running of that market. Although a "spiritual" approach to life might seem to depend on "soft knowledge" and a "technological" approach on "hard knowledge," there are intangibles and unknowns on both sides. In an interesting and original analysis, Taylor speaks of the ethical problems of human cloning in terms of the unprecedented complexities it creates for the clone. Taylor said that "who you are is who you relate to and how you see yourself. We need to think of the clone in terms of the complexity of the situation that we have created for the clone — no father or mother, no sense that he or she was produced through sex, and so on."

Might our refusal to accept complexity, which might be an effort to control uncertainty and thereby reduce our fear of the unknown and the anxiety that produces, paradoxically have backfired and resulted in the creation of a culture of anxiety? It is said that in order to be in denial, a person must have an awareness of the matter denied in order to keep it repressed. Repression uses up large amounts of psychic energy and can result in depression. Might we have placed our collective psyche in denial about complexity, and in doing so created a social climate of anxiety, fear, and depression?

• • •

This is the point in the Massey Lectures where I'm supposed to pull it all together and deliver the "master plan." I've decided to take a different route, however, and look at some of the human qualities that I believe will be essential in taking ethical paths into our human future. Let's consider some "old virtues" and how we see them today. The qualities I look at are trust, courage, compassion, generosity, and hope. And, finally, I want to talk about the deep human desire for home.

Trust

"Confidence in or reliance on some quality or attribute of a person or thing, or the truth of a statement. . . . Confident expectation of something; hope. . . . The obligation or responsibility imposed on one in whom confidence is placed or authority is vested, or who has given an undertaking of fidelity."
— Oxford English Dictionary

Many people believe that there has been a decline of trust in our societies, but in some respects we trust more now than in the past. Today we eat food that comes from the other side of the world and that has passed through the hands of countless strangers. Consider what your great-grandmother knew about the origins and handling of the food she ate for breakfast, compared with what we know about ours. On the other hand, authority figures such as politicians, judges, and police may not be any more or less trustworthy than in the past, but we now know more about what they do, and we do not simply, automatically trust people in authority. We have changed from having blind trust in authority figures ("trust me because I have status, power, and authority and will act in your 'best interests' and look after you") to requiring such authorities to earn our trust ("trust me because I will show that you can trust me and will continue to earn your trust").[4]

Because "blind trust" is based on power, status, and authority, it is paternalistic in nature. "Earned trust" is based on being trustworthy and is egalitarian in nature. The change from "blind trust" to "earned trust" has occurred at both individual and societal levels, although the change at the societal level can easily be misinterpreted as merely a loss of trust rather than a change in the nature of the trust. It is true that the public's trust in authority figures has declined. But that might simply reflect the change from blind trust to earned trust. Indeed, there may be more earned trust today than in the past when our (blind) trust was often unmerited by those in whom we placed it.

Our general loss of trust as a society might also be the result of our rejection of the exercise of authority. As well, because of the impact of modern media and communications technologies, some authority figures are seen to be less trustworthy than in the past. And in fact, some authorities might indeed be less trustworthy than they were in the past. Recently in Canada, we have seen several official inquiries into situations that have involved breach of public trust — for instance, the Krever Inquiry into HIV contamination of the blood system, and the Gomery Commission looking into the use of public money for political payoffs. In a remarkable counter-example of trust-inspiring behaviour, the Honourable Monique Bégin, former minister of health of Canada, waived her ministerial right to immunity before the Krever Inquiry. The public's response was overwhelming. Bégin was swamped with faxes, voicemail, email, and letters saying, "Thank God, at last a politician has taken responsibility and stood up to be counted, at risk to herself."

Lack of trust in politics is not one-sided. Politicians don't trust the public to be wise enough to hear the truth. More and more, politicians govern according to what the polls tell them the public wants — whether or not what they want is possible or for the good — and communicate predominantly through publicist-prepared sound bites.[5] The resulting loss of authenticity, integrity, and spontaneity is tragic. The public perceives this loss through their "other ways of knowing" — a perception that polls based just on "hard evidence," reason, and statistics might not reflect. These perceptions can affect people's decision-making, especially, I suggest, in real situations such as voting as compared to hypothetical ones such as surveys on voting. This might help to explain why pollsters are finding an increasing number of undecided voters until just before ballots are cast.[6]

The word *integrity* often comes up in discussions of politicians and trust. The *Oxford English Dictionary* defines moral integrity as an "unimpaired moral state; freedom from moral corruption; innocence . . . soundness of moral principle." In 2005, integrity was the most frequently searched word in *Webster's On-Line Dictionary*. Integrity is at the heart of ethics and a *sine qua non* of all the other virtues in our personal and communal lives. Integrity and its opposite, corruption, are contagious. We can imagine corruption as the moral equivalent of a cancer-causing virus. It eats out the vital organs of organizations, institutions, and even the state itself. Democracy, justice, respect for human rights, and ethical conduct die as a result. We often identify corruption as the primary cause of such outcomes, but we might gain insights by seeing it as secondary to the loss of integrity. That change might allow us to design remedies that otherwise might not be obvious.

Might we, as a society, have lost trust because we are now unable to trust anything we can't experience directly with our senses — we trust only what we can see or hear or touch? And might we have lost it because we now also have virtual reality, which means things that are not real can seem real to our senses? I wonder if, in the past, religious belief might have helped us to develop the capacity to trust what is not accessible to our senses. Those with faith in religion learned to have this kind of trust from the time they were young children. Assuming we have lost trust in intangible realities, how might this affect our ability to pass on values? Perhaps young people will not trust values if they do not trust intangibles. Moreover, it may now be equally difficult for us to trust what we *can* perceive with our senses. So many things that we see cannot be trusted — for example, video footage shown on television or in documentary films is sometimes faked or reconstructed. Media reports and documentaries must be held to a high standard of truth if we as a society are not to lose trust. Societal trust is difficult to establish, fragile, and easy to destroy. It is lost by thousands of small cuts to its integrity, not by one major event. The ethical challenge is to establish a culture of trust, and to do that we must restore our faith in a basic presumption of truth.

In our personal relationships, we can consider friendship a prime example of a pure and important form of trust. But friendship used in the wrong context or wrong way (nepotism, or for political advantage) becomes a serious breach of trust. This is an example of a "mixed ethical system" causing ethical problems: the different "moral syndromes" or systems that govern friendship and politics each has its own internal integrity and rules[7], but when these syndromes are mixed, abuse occurs in both directions — that is, abuse of friendship and of political power.

In both personal and societal relationships, there is a link between trust and control: we are willing to give up control if we trust; we refuse to do so if we cannot trust. Being able to give up control is as necessary as being able to take control if we are to find balance in many situations we face in our lives. It allows others to govern for the benefit of the society, allows others to take care of us when we are old, ill, or disabled, and makes it possible for us to die peacefully. Henry Emerson Fosdick puts it this way: "He who cannot rest, cannot work; he who cannot let go, cannot hold on; he who cannot find footing, cannot go forward."

Here I will pose a simple question that has no simple answers, and that links trust, courage, and hope: Can we trust the future? I mentioned the concept of obligations to future generations previously, although some people reject the idea that we have any such obligations. But surely an ethics of responsibility requires that we ask ourselves this, at the very least: What obligations do we owe future generations if we are to hold human life on trust for them? If we are to act ethically toward future generations, what limits should we impose on ourselves now?

Jürgen Habermas responds to that question once again when discussing new reproductive technologies.[8] He says that our actions in using new technoscience must not deprive future generations of life-fulfilling human experiences by depriving them of innate capacities for self-actualization, of a sense of autonomy, and of the personal freedom necessary to realize their own selves and lives in ways that are available to us. Without naming them as such, Habermas proposes we use some moral "limiting devices" to guide our decisions about the new technoscience. He invites us to "adopt the perspective of a future present from which we might someday perhaps look back on currently controversial practices,"[9] and to be warned by what we anticipate might happen. In short, he warns of the "slippery slope" dangers of reprogenetic technologies — in particular the danger that seeing some interventions as ethically acceptable will necessarily lead us to embrace ethically unacceptable forms of intervention. In other words, we must be careful which doors we open to reproductive technologies to ensure we are not heading down a path to unethical outcomes from which there is no turning back. In this sense, honouring trust can require that we place limits on tolerance, because exceeding those limits would involve a breach of trust.

A related concept proposed by Habermas is what he calls "assumed consent"[10] or an "anticipated no."[11] In intervening on human embryos, we must be able to assume one of two things: either that whatever we do to them, they would retrospectively consent to what we did; or if we discard them, that the unborn person would have said no to the burden of suffering life would have entailed — that is, would have said "no" to life. The latter reflects the argument on which "wrongful life" cases are based: that being alive — life itself — is a damage for which the child should be compensated. Accepting such a claim requires a court to acknowledge that no life would have been better for the plaintiff than the life the plaintiff has — that is, that the plaintiff would be better off dead. This is a highly controversial claim that the vast majority of courts have rejected.[12] Rightly, in my view.

One way to express Habermas's view of the new genetics if they were to become the new *eugenics* — a word I use here in its unethical sense — is as a new form of slavery of, and tyranny over, others in the future by those in the past. In milder terms, we can express the same idea as a serious failure to respect intergenerational equality. Those who were not designed, and as a result have "genetic freedom," are designing children who will lack such freedom. This is unjust — a failure to implement "justice across the generations."[13] Justice and trust are linked. We rightly don't — indeed, can't — trust those from whom we rightly fear injustice. And breach of trust is a form of injustice. This should lead us to think about what we hold on trust for others, or should hold on trust for them — for instance, the human germ-cell line. To breach that trust is also a failure to implement justice across the generations.

I have already mentioned Kazuo Ishiguro's novel *Never Let Me Go*[14] in an earlier chapter. It powerfully communicates why we must hold human life on trust for future generations and not use the new technoscience in any way that breaches that trust. Through the slow and deliberate ordinariness of the world Ishiguro creates, we come to see the appalling harm — indeed, the evil — done to designed persons, in this case clones created as future tissue- and organ-donors. In the novel, these cloned persons do not refuse to be donors, although it will mean their deaths when vital organs are taken. Left unsaid is why that is the case. I believe it is because the designed humans cannot perceive of themselves as free or autonomous, and they certainly don't see themselves as equal to others. It is ironic that in an age of intense individualism we are developing reproductive technologies that could be used by those claiming individual rights to "reproductive autonomy" to carry out the most egregious breaches of the most fundamental human rights of the children who result. Likewise, those who oppose placing ethical limits on medical technologies that promise breakthrough cures for horrible diseases see their rights to such cures as trumping any harms involved in developing them.

The concept of our having obligations to "hold certain entities on trust for future generations" is related to hope. As I discuss later in this chapter, hope is generated by a sense of connection to the future. The idea and reality of "holding on trust for future generations" embodies both hope for us and for those future generations. It allows us to see ourselves as connected to the future — one we will not see — through the intact legacy we leave behind. This elicits hope in us. And seeing ourselves as having obligations to protect what future humans need to generate hope for themselves and their descendants will preserve the conditions in which they, too, can find hope.

Finally, I want to link doubt to trust. As I've suggested before, doubt is the shadow side of faith — we only have doubt if we have faith — and certainty is the opposite of both. Trust is a form of faith. Many people have placed their faith and trust in science and technology, for instance. The danger is that they believe science and technology can fix all problems. We must maintain a healthy doubt in that regard if we are not to go astray ethically.

Courage

"That quality of mind which shows itself in facing danger without fear or shrinking; bravery, boldness, valour. . . . The heart as the seat of feeling, thought, etc.; spirit, mind, disposition, nature."

— Oxford English Dictionary

Huntington's Disease is a horrible, inherited, genetic disease that results in loss of mental competency and death in midlife. All people with the gene develop the disease — there is no window of escape. In March 1995, I heard a woman who had been diagnosed with the Huntington's Disease gene interviewed on CBC Radio. She quietly said: "My goal is not so much to beat it, as to not let it beat me." This is an example of enormous courage. Note that in her approach, this woman accepts the reality of what her diagnosis means, she is not in denial, and she sees herself as primary, not the disease.

Unlike this woman, many sick people become their illnesses. For instance, after a myocardial infarction (a heart attack), many people ask, "Who am I?" And they often respond, "I am a heart attack; I am *my* heart attack." They no longer see themselves as persons. Some doctors refer to a myocardial infarction as an ego infarction. For the person who has experienced it, it raises questions such as: How will I be viewed? Will I be acceptable, desirable? Will I matter? Another way to deal with our own illness is to view everyone as being ill. As one physician put it, "The well are only the undiagnosed sick" — even if most of us, for most of our lives, live with the illusion that there is nothing wrong with us. These different responses show that it takes courage to deal with illness, whether we bolster that courage through religion, as many people did in the past, or medicine, as many people now do.

The virtue of courage can be linked to that of restraint. The law has a very old saying that applies to protecting liberty: it speaks of "freedom in fetters." We must exercise restraint, and sometimes even use the law to restrict liberty, when such restriction is essential to protect the conditions that make freedom possible. It can take far more courage to say no to the current "received wisdom," and especially to speak truth to power, than to say yes. Courage can be manifested both in acting and in not acting, although the former is often more readily identified as courage. Still, in some cultures the man who turns his back to a threat and walks away from a fight is seen as courageous and strong. The same can be true in sport. In mountaineering culture, the sign of a great alpinist is not someone who always reaches the summit, but the person who is able to turn back when faced with a great threat of danger. Wisdom and restraint can be essential elements of courage; they are the flip side of the courage to fight for what we believe in when what we believe in is threatened and it is right to fight against that threat. Societies and individuals need both forms of courage — that is, the courage to act when action is the ethical response to a threat or challenge, and the courage to refrain from acting when such restraint is called for. Indeed, one way to test the ethics of a society is by what it chooses *not* to do, although action might be of some benefit; in other words, the ethics of a society can be measured by the strength of the virtue of restraint it manifests. Our approach to human embryo stem-cell research, which was discussed previously, is an important, current, controversial test case in this regard.

Leadership, when undertaken ethically, is often a concrete manifestation of courage. CBC-TV made a documentary about a Canadian doctor, Dr. Chandra Sankurathri, who was born in India of Indian ancestry and who lost his wife and two children — his entire immediate family — in the Air India tragedy of 1985, in which terrorists blew up a plane.[15] Dr. Sankurathri mourned his loss, and then decided to return to India to help those most in need — old people who were going blind but whose sight could be restored with surgery, and children who had no access to education. Watching the documentary was a profoundly moving experience. My thoughts were of the contrast between the powerful "quiet leadership" of this courageous and humble man of great integrity — a wounded healer, someone who had turned his own suffering into a force for good for others — and that of so many so-called "star leaders," who seem to have no substance, no humility, no purpose other than self-aggrandizement and holding on to power, and no integrity or principles other than doing what polls and spin doctors tell them is saleable to the public.

Speaking truth to power, as ethics requires, and trying to make those who exercise power understand what that truth demands of them ethically, both call for moral courage. Courage is absent when we choose power over truth, especially when we are untrue to our own most authentic selves and beliefs.

Courage is demanded when dealing with risk, whether the risk is physical or moral. One temptation for people in authority is to minimize or disguise risks that, if disclosed, could cause them difficulties or harm their authority in some way. We see examples of this when politicians, bureaucrats, health-care professionals, engineers, or architects make mistakes that seriously harm others. In these situations, having the courage to be forthright, frank, and honest is essential. Ironically, being courageous is likely to minimize the retribution or penalty that the wrongdoer faces. When physicians admit to medical negligence and say they're sorry, they're much less likely to be sued. Metaphysical and moral risks sometimes require even more courage to face. Standing up for values that we believe in, especially when they are derided or rejected by others, or when doing so can cost us loving relationships or friends or family or employment, or when we become the target of shaming, exclusion, or bullying, can be deeply emotionally traumatizing.

Stigmatizing those with whom we disagree, especially as a strategy to promote our own views over those of the person or group stigmatized, is especially uncourageous. It is the opposite of speaking truth to power. Rather, it is a means of escaping or avoiding the truth at the expense of a scapegoated person or group. It is an exercise in reducing our guilt for treating others in a way that would appall us if we were treated that way ourselves, by sharing that guilt with fellow stigmatizers — an indication that not only misery, but also cowardice, needs company. Some contemporary advocacy groups, such as identity-based social movements, especially single-issue ones, need to take care that in promoting their cause they do not use tactics that result in people being afraid to speak truth to power.

Finally, we need the courage to stand by our ethical beliefs, even when we are at odds with the majority of others in our society in doing so. Some research by philosophers of science in Australia should give us hope in this regard. These philosophers used computers to establish large sequential decision-making sets of 5,000 or 10,000 consecutive decisions. In this experiment, they divided up the computer screen into small squares, half of them red and half yellow. They called each red square a "rat" and each yellow square a "lemming." The computer was programmed so that each rat decided only in its own self-interest while the lemmings only made decisions that were in everyone's best interest. At first, the yellow-square lemmings were quickly reduced in number as the red-square rats took over. But the researchers found that as long as a small clustered group of lemmings remained and did not fall below a critical mass, eventually the lemmings would come back, springing up here and there and regaining strength.[16] There is an important and hopeful message in this: A few voices crying in the ethical wilderness do matter and can prevail, even in the face of overwhelming odds.

Compassion

"Suffering together with another, participation in suffering; fellow-feeling, sympathy. . . . The feeling or emotion, when a person is moved by the suffering or distress of another, and by the desire to relieve it; pity that inclines one to spare or to succour."
— Oxford English Dictionary

Compassion and courage are companions. To be compassionate we must stand in the shoes of the other. That takes courage when what we see in the other, and what requires our compassion, makes us terrified that we could suffer the same fate. Compassion is concern for others. It is the "golden rule" — to treat others as we would want to be treated, and not treat others as we would not wish to be treated — that forms the base of the world's great religions. Historian of world religions Karen Armstrong believes that we need "to recover the lost heart of compassion that lies at the centre of all our great world religions." These religions have always accepted, she says, that the best way for their adherents to rid themselves of ego is by compassion — the idea that when you give yourself away in compassion, you become stronger. And, she explains, these religions' advocacy of the "golden rule" was intended to elicit compassion that extended to everyone, not just to one's own group. The rule also encouraged people to use their own past pain to understand and thereby avoid inflicting pain on others. Interestingly, Armstrong believes that compassion also allows a person to experience the sacred. Earlier, I proposed a concept I called the *secular sacred*. So if compassion allows us to experience the religious sacred, might it also help us to experience the secular sacred? In any case, we should give much thought to Armstrong's conclusion that a major problem with religions today is that "many religious people prefer to be right, rather than compassionate."[17] Religion can and must, however, be both right *and* compassionate.

Compassion is closely linked to ethics, which may mean that "compassion fatigue" (when people become apathetic or indifferent toward the suffering of others as the demands on them to be compassionate, especially financial demands by charities, become too great) leads to "ethics fatigue." If so, we need to guard against this. The possibility of "ethics fatigue," or ethics burnout, leads us to the concept of *moricide* — that is, "moral suicide," which means that as individuals, communities, and societies we intentionally kill off our moral sensibility because we feel that we can no longer cope ethically. Recognizing such a concept could alert us to moral dangers that we would not otherwise perceive because we had eliminated our sensitivity to them.

Empathy (the ability to vicariously experience another's feelings) elicits compassion. Because our society values reason so highly, we need to be aware that reason unmodified by other ways of knowing may block empathy and compassion. The climbers who walked past a dying fellow climber on Mount Everest displayed such a blockage. They seemed to have reasoned that they could not save their comrade's life, so there was no point in abandoning their goal of reaching the summit. Their decision does not appear to have been informed by empathy, compassion or moral intuition, for that would have resulted in a different outcome: the climbers would not have abandoned a fellow human to die alone.[18]

Psychologists have identified a phenomenon called "moral disengagement." Here's how it was described in a *New York Times* article: ". . . [P]eople's moral codes are more flexible than generally understood. To buffer themselves from their own consciences, people often adjust their moral judgements in a process some psychologists call moral disengagement, or moral distancing. . . . Moral disengagement 'is our ability to selectively engage and disengage our moral standards, and it helps explain how people can be barbarically cruel in one moment and compassionate the next.'"[19] In short, moral disengagement blocks a compassionate response and, I propose, an ethical one. Psychologically deprogramming soldiers before they engage in hand-to-hand combat is one example of the routine, deliberate eliciting of this response. It is important for us to be aware of this phenomenon if we are to act ethically.

At the same time, we should also be aware of pseudo virtues, including pseudo-compassion. This is comprised of lots of compassionate talk, but a failure to act that is necessary for true compassion. The serious danger is that a combination of "pseudos" (such as pseudo virtues) with "intense's" (such as intense individualism, or intense capitalism, or single-issue advocacy groups — any positions that are so polarized they exclude considerations on the other side) can lead to an ethically void, and morally, spiritually, and emotionally impoverished world. Worrying as individual examples of a "pseudo" or an "intense" are, they are of far greater concern in combination because they interact synergistically, not simply cumulatively. These "pseudo-intense" combinations can have devastating effect on our collective societal values.[20] "Marketplace ethics" is an example. The concept is based on intense capitalism, argues for personal freedom of choice as a virtue, and promotes the idea that what is and is not ethical should be decided entirely by consumer choice. The theory is that because consumers are ethical, they will not buy unethical products or services, which will therefore fail commercially. So there is no need to regulate genetic or reproductive technologies, for example, to ensure that they are used ethically. This is a "good for business" approach to ethics.

A contemporary example of the opposite approach — of practically incorporating compassion into societal values — is found in the call to build an "ethic of care" into the fabric of society, which is a central theme of many feminist movements and feminist ethics.[21] In the past, an "ethic of care" was conveyed to us through religion and the concept of charity, which was integral to the fabric of, for example, Judaism and Christianity. Once again, the issue we face now is: How do we put into practice such values in secular societies?

Perhaps another question — What do we want for ourselves and society, and how do compassion and charity fit into those goals? — will help us to respond to the former question. In addressing the first part of our question —

what do we want? — some people have answered that we want love, friendship, and freedom of thought. The theologian Thomas Merton lists spirit, spirituality, community, society, religion, and bonding, because these are all ways of searching for meaning, and ultimately, Merton believes, what we want is meaning. He proposes that we should not seek happiness — or at least not directly. He also includes in his list kindness, grace, forgiveness, and redemption. Note that all these entities are aspects of compassion; we also might ask whether they are unique marks of being human. I believe they all are — but the same might not be true of an entity we discussed earlier, empathy. Recent research reported by neuropsychologist Jeffrey Mogil's McGill University laboratory shows that mice exhibit empathy for other mice in pain;[22] this makes the question of whether empathy is unique to humans open to doubts that we would never have had in the past.

Other relatively recent research, this time into humans, shows that the brain pattern of people who see someone in pain changes to more closely mimic the brain pattern they would have if they themselves were in pain. In this sense, we could say — and I have long believed this to be true from anecdotal observation — that pain exhibits some characteristics of being contagious. It is not uncommon for people to find it extremely difficult to stay with someone in serious pain. Yet other research purportedly shows that empathy for a person in pain can differ between men and women. A brain-scanning study suggests that when men see a cheater get a mild electric shock, they don't feel his pain much at all. In fact, they rather enjoy it. In contrast, the scanning of women's brains showed they do empathize with the cheater's pain and do not get a kick out it.[23]

Such research needs careful scrutiny for bias, whether accidental or deliberate — some cultural studies researchers see it as being biased toward women as "good" people and against men as "bad" people. But if it holds up, it once again shows that the more that we learn through our extraordinary new science, the more we know how much we don't know.

To return to the question of whether empathy is a uniquely human characteristic: Unlike people, whose brains show an empathetic response to both intimates and strangers (although empathy is stronger towards intimates), mice only respond to those with whom they have had social contact. Perhaps, then, the unique human characteristic is being able to empathize with strangers, not just our own "mob," which brings us back to the "Golden Rule."

Generosity

"Willingness to lay aside resentment or forgive injuries; magnanimity. . . . Readiness or liberality in giving; munificence."
— Oxford English Dictionary

We can well ask where justice ends and generosity begins. Take access to health care, for example. Ninety percent of the world's population has access to only ten percent of the world's health-care resources. We tolerate people dying from diseases that are easy to prevent or treat, including forty thousand children a day dying for lack of minimal health care and of preventable causes, including starvation. That is a failure both of justice and of generosity. What can be done about these situations?

It seems that direct appeals to justice and generosity largely fall on deaf ears. Perhaps what we need is a more indirect, diverse, and nuanced inquiry into "ways and means" that might elicit a humane response. We need to generate insights that will awaken us —which is what insights do. We must learn to speak in a way that allows us to come alive ethically and as a result respond to injustice with generosity. And we must identify and dismantle the current barriers to that occurring.

For instance, we could examine whether consumerism — buying goods solely for the sake of buying and having them — is one such barrier. Consumerism is a cherished value in a technocratic society — people value the acquisition of technology and their own reliance on it, especially when this is characterized as improving their standard of living. But there is an important difference between standard of living and quality of life. Increased productivity and its companion, increased consumerism, augments the former but not necessarily the latter. Perhaps we need to move from a mantra of "more is better" to "enough is best," even if we put the latter into practice only some of the time. Liberating the marketplace does not necessarily liberate people; indeed, it can have the opposite effect. The associated danger, of which we are seeing more and more evidence, especially in the use of new medical and reproductive technologies, is the commodification of all our human engagements with one another — our most intimate personal interactions are being transformed into transactions. Commodification indisputably happens when human embryos are created for the purpose of using them as the source of therapeutic products, a topic discussed earlier. It also can be present when we pass on life to our children if that occurs through services made available by the "fertility industry." This industry is raising a great number and wide variety of important ethical issues in many countries. But some of the most deeply troubling ethical issues we face involve reproductive tourism in countries such as India, where poverty-stricken women are selling their ova and acting as surrogate mothers for people from developed countries who can afford to pay the "middlemen" who are the main financial beneficiaries. Ironically, the fertility industry often uses the concept of generosity, under the guise of being generous to infertile people, as a recruitment and marketing tool, probably because the cloak of altruism the presence of generosity provides is ethically reassuring and dulls troubling moral intuitions.

What themes or concepts might we explore for insights that could stimulate our true generosity toward others, or remove barriers to it? Let's begin by examining the differences between inclusiveness and exclusiveness.

Multiculturalism is one way to promote inclusiveness and to avoid excluding others. But we must consider what we mean by multiculturalism and what we want it to be — in short, we must define it. It can be understood to mean the lowest common denominator among a broadly diverse group of people, or it can mean a rich tapestry in which each part is different but contributes to a whole. We must also identify multiculturalism's goals, because it is not an end in itself. I suggest those goals should include holism (and therefore we must be careful to avoid fragmentation of society in implementing multiculturalism) and integrity (and therefore we must strive for wholeness of being, something that will require imaginative measures). Implementing multiculturalism requires judgement (good judgement is essential in the inevitable conflict of concerns and principles that will arise). The policy's dangers include confusing respect for diversity with cultural relativism — that is, a belief that all cultures and values are of equal worth. Our overall challenge is to find consensus that is strong enough to bind us together to form a society in which we all feel we belong, while recognizing diversity and difference. In this discussion, the responsibilities and restraints of hospitality, which I discuss shortly, are relevant considerations.

In a recent review of *Identity and Violence: The Illusion of Destiny* by Amartya Sen, and of *Cosmopolitanism* by Kwame Anthony Appiah, theologian Lorenzo DiTommaso distinguishes cosmopolitanism, pluralism, and universalism. He says that for both Sen and Appiah, the key to living more peacefully with our "myriad differences . . . is understanding one's neighbours." Appiah, he says, "urges us to become more 'cosmopolitan' (in the full knowledge of the term's historical connotations), which implies that we recognize our obligations to our fellow humans, not just to the members of our community or country, and which demands taking seriously other cultures, practices and beliefs. Cosmopolitanism is not pluralism, since despite its good intentions, pluralism sees communities and cultures tectonically. Nor is it universalism, which tends to view differences as something to be overcome. As Appiah puts it, cosmopolitanism is universalism plus differences: a recognition that we are all human and so share human things, but that we also are different, too, and that these differences are important."[24] There is much to contemplate here in the search for a shared ethics which also must encompass universals *and* differences within an integrated, stable but consistently evolving whole.

Making judgements about what should and should not be tolerated as part of a multicultural society can lead one into dangerous territory, not least the danger of offending those with strong stances or certain values. Perhaps we might view these judgements differently if we characterized making them as a responsibility — and not as the exercise of any right or entitlement to impose our views and values on others who might disagree with them. Defining values in a multicultural society is a delicate and sensitive undertaking, and is an ongoing process, not an event that occurs once and is finished.

Multiculturalism is a response to immigrants and immigrant communities. How we view such people individually and collectively, and how we view their rights and claims on us, can radically affect what we expect from them and how we treat them. Under international law, entry to a country of which one is not a national is a privilege, not a right — except in the case of refugees whose lives are in danger.[25] This means that, on the whole, we see ourselves as being generous in allowing immigration; we are less likely to characterize ourselves as being just in doing so. This is an important distinction because rightly or wrongly, we do not see ourselves as having a duty to be generous; we're more likely to see ourselves as having a duty to be just. Likewise, if we see ourselves as being generous in allowing immigration, we are likely to feel more justified in imposing conditions on immigrants — for instance, requiring them to accept our values and adapt to our culture. Generosity is primarily an emotional response; justice is more often a reasoned response, perhaps because we use law, which is based on reason, as the main means of remedying injustice in many of our societies. We need to explore such differences if we are to gain insights that could help us to respond ethically to the kinds of cultural clashes that have recently become part of the "normal" urban landscape in many contemporary Western societies.

One such insight in suggested by Washington, D.C. freelance writer Lynda McDaniel in an article entitled "The Recklessly Generous Heart." McDaniel explains that "[h]ospitality is not a flurry of sentimental acts or occasional gestures. It is a sustained commitment to the belief that the way we treat one another day by day matters deeply."[26] The tradition of hospitality is embedded in the monastic life — for the monks, attending to the needs of the guest took priority over work and even prayer. We can contemplate what is the contemporary equivalent of "putting a cloak on somebody's back as you go [by them] or giving them food or water."[27]

It is important to point out here that respect is a mutual undertaking, not a one-way street. Immigrants also ought to consider what respect for their host country requires and behave accordingly. The guest in the monastery was not allowed to burn down the abbey or to assault the monks and was expected to show respect for "the rules of the Order." Such respect did not require the guest personally to adopt those rules, but it did require that he or she not disrespect or transgress the values of the hosts. In short, hosts and guests had reciprocal obligations, and mutual respect and courtesy were no mere formalities.

Exploring generosity in the form of hospitality can offer other other insights. The philosopher Immanuel Kant spoke of "the universal law of hospitality"[28] and the theologian Henri Nouwen described hospitality as "the creation of a space where the stranger can enter and become a friend instead of an enemy." That space is not just a physical one, but also a mental one. Open-mindedness is extending hospitality to the ideas of others, and it mediates respect for those others; closed-mindedness is the opposite in both regards. Open-mindedness is a willingness to entertain others' ideas and consider them, not necessarily to accept or adopt them. We need to be careful, however, not to confuse socially liberal values with open-mindedness and socially conservative ones with closed-mindedness, as often seems to happen. People can be socially liberal and closed-minded, or socially conservative and open-minded. In short, hospitality is manifested in both open doors and open minds. Hospitality is a form of behaviour and a process, not just an attitude or a static state.

Perhaps, if we kept in mind the words of the poet Emily Dickinson, we might treat others more generously. Dickinson writes:

> If I can stop one heart from breaking,
> I shall not live in vain;
> If I can ease one life the aching,
> Or cool one pain,
> Or help one fainting robin
> Unto his nest again,
> I shall not live in vain.[29]

Hope

"Expectation of something desired; desire combined with expectation. . . . A person or thing that gives hope or promise for the future, or in which hopes are centred."

— Oxford English Dictionary

Hope is linked to many of the other entities I have discussed in this chapter, and may be foundational to other virtues. For instance, courage can be linked to hope. Indeed, sometimes courage is necessary if we are to find hope. As we discussed earlier, hope requires a sense of connection to the future, but that future does not have to be a distant one. For instance, a dying person can find hope in looking forward to a planned visit from an old friend in a few hours' time. Research has shown that the difference between one group of people with amyotrophic lateral sclerosis (ALS, or Lou Gehrig's disease) who wanted euthanasia, and another group who did not, was not the presence or absence of depression but the presence or absence of a condition the research psychiatrists call hopelessness, a condition they were able to distinguish from depression.[30] The main indicator of hopelessness was that the people who suffered from it believed they had nothing to live for, nothing to look forward to.

Because hope is linked to the future, it's linked to potentiality. For this reason, the ethics of potentiality and the idea that it can be ethically wrong to deliberately negate potential are relevant to the discussion of hope. We can describe hope as a sense of possibility — the sense that our best dreams, no matter how short-term they might be, are open to fulfillment. Helping others to find hope requires imagination and creativity on the part of individuals, institutions, and societies; our enemies in this enterprise are apathy, boredom, inactivity, and nihilism. I believe that acting in ways that cause such a loss of passion should be viewed as an ethical "mortal sin."

I also believe it's a mistake to perceive hope as passive. Rather we can compare "making hope" with making war or making peace. It is probable that hope is contagious. As I mentioned earlier, we now know that the brain patterns of people who are physically close to people in pain mimic those they would have if they themselves were in pain, which might partially explain why it is so difficult to witness another person in pain.[31] Might it also be true that we mimic the brain patterns of people "in hope"?

Hope is a human good. It is real, but it is not a physical reality, not a scientific fact, and not necessarily based on reason (although it is not antithetical to reason). It simply belongs to a different order of realities. We can argue that it is inherently wrong to intentionally destroy hope — which is what torture does, and is the means through which torture works. Torture makes the present reality of pain the only reality for the tortured person — the person becomes the pain. Consequently, no matter how much "good" might be done by torturing a person, it is inherently wrong to do so. It's worth noting that we reach this conclusion of inherent wrongness by agreeing on a common "good" — hope — and by agreeing that it is inherently wrong to destroy that "good," and not by basing our arguments on moral relativity, nor by relying on an appeal to a moral authority such as God or religion.

Throughout this book I have looked at the necessity of finding a shared ethics, of deciding what the shared base of that ethics might consist of, and of determining how we might find it. One way of doing this I have not yet expressly mentioned is to search for essential human "goods" (like hope) on which we can agree — even if we can't agree on the full range of what constitutes those goods. Finding those goods might bridge gaps between us, including those between utilitarian ethicists and principle-based ones. American philosopher Richard Rorty, a utilitarian, suggests "social hope" is such a good. I agree.

Hope and the search for meaning in life are linked, in that each helps us to find the other (another example of the snake swallowing its tail). They are also linked in that the absence of either has the same impact on us: without meaning or without hope, we believe that we cannot go on living.

Robert F. Kennedy linked hope and justice, saying:

> Each time a person stands up for an ideal or acts to improve the lot of others or strikes out against injustice, they send forth a tiny ripple of hope, and crossing each other from a million different centers of energy and daring, these ripples build a current that can sweep down the mightiest walls of oppression and resistance.[32]

Hope as a basis for a shared ethics raises the question: Is searching for hope a religious pursuit or a secular one, or can it be both? Religion gives us one way to find hope. But many people are now also looking for new ways to find hope in our secular societies. I suggest that hope seems to be intrinsically connected with religion — in the broad sense of that word, where it implies bonding — because we appear to be turning some of these relatively newer ways of seeking hope into secular religions — for example, scientism and atheism. Just as traditional religion is dangerous when it becomes moralism (which I define as morality practised impersonally, without sympathy or empathy, and to the exclusion of other relevant considerations), scientism and atheism are dangerous when they become secular moralism. Historian Gil Troy says that in today's world, individualism has trumped moralism.[33] But the danger is that sometimes the new "religion" of individualism may also trump morality.

While not abandoning religion for those who find hope through it, I believe we need to explore where and how we can find hope other than through religion. I have written elsewhere that hope is the oxygen of the human spirit: without it, our human spirit dies; with it, we can survive appalling suffering and surmount incredible obstacles.[34] A statement attributed to Saint Augustine might explain why hope functions for our spirit in that way. He said, "Hope has two lovely daughters: anger and courage. Anger so that what must not be may not be; courage so that what should be can be." Those emotions cause us to engage with the world and doing so nourishes our human spirit — life and what we do with it matters to us and others, that is, we find meaning. Reciprocally, we must have a sense of the human spirit if we are to have the capacity to find hope. The issue is, how can we nurture that capacity?

I understand evolutionary biologist and futurist Elisabet Sahtouris to be addressing this question when she writes:

Recognizing our responsibility and opportunity for *creating* our reality is the only way I see for making the shift from fear to love—from a world of scarcity and greed to one of abundance in which all people are empowered to fulfil their needs in sustainable ways. To achieve this, we must break through long cultural conditioning on our lack of power, our willingness to accept, and thus co-create, economic and political inequities that disempower people, currency systems that promote these inequities and anything else preventing the full expression of human potential in sustainable ways.[35]

Sahtouris is speaking from an altruistic point of view, but even if we were to adopt a selfish point of view, creating the possibility of hope for others may be the best — or perhaps the only — way to find hope for ourselves, especially if we are to leave a legacy of hope for our children and their children.

Hope for one's children has been a primary experience for most people across the generations. In the modern era in the West, it has taken the form of parents hoping that their children will be more prosperous and successful than they were. For the first time in recent memory, Western parents are being told that they should expect their children to be less well off economically than they are. One response to this situation is to lose hope. Another is to refocus hope away from material values to postmaterial, posteconomic ones, such as fostering loving relationships with family and friends, caring for animals and the environment, and actively participating in the arts and cultural events. Even if parents are not doing that — at least not yet — there are signs that postmaterial values might be growing among young people. Ironically, the parents' loss of a way to access hope (through the expectation of greater economic prosperity for their children) might increase the children's access to a sense of hope.

Poets and artists, prophets and mystics have often metaphorically linked hope to breath, air, feathers, the spirit, and the source of life. The great Christian mystic nun Hildegard von Bingen called her music, which embodies hope, "a feather floating on the breath of God." As breathing is for the body, hope is for the human spirit. Just as we must continuously breathe in and breathe out to go on living — breathing in being the active phase and breathing out the passive phase — we constantly need both to seek hope and to allow it to come to us. Personal trainers and yoga instructors teach us to breathe out as we make maximum physical effort in the gym or practise yoga, thus keeping our lungs optimally inflated and allowing air to flow in. In just this way, we must make a maximum effort to expel despair, thus keeping our human spirit "optimally inflated" and opening up space within ourselves so that hope can flow in. At times of greatest despair, we may simply need to remain open to hope and allow it to come to us. At other times, we must deliberately seek or imagine a beneficient future in order to connect to it, thereby generating hope.

Finally, the mathematician and cosmologist Brian Swimme captures the soul of hope in an indirect, beautiful, poetic, and unusual way when he says: "Just think: four billion years ago the earth was molten rock, now it sings opera."[36]

Coming Home

Some people respond to the question, What do we want? (or, What do we need?) with the answer: A sense of belonging — to a place, and to something larger than ourselves. These people are expressing the need within all of us to experience transcendence. Transcendence requires us to feel that we have a physical home and an emotional home as individuals and as members of a community that embraces us — one in which we can experience transcendence.[37]

Attachment to a place can be contrasted with the longing for adventure. We need both; we need balance. Glenn Albrecht speaks of two concepts — nostalgia and solacestalgia — that embody our feelings of loss when a place that is important to our emotional well-being disappears. Nostalgia is a sense of loss of one's home, and a longing for that lost place. Solacestalgia (a term Albrecht coined) is a sense of the destruction (for instance, by environmental damage) of our place and home and the solace it provided even while we remain in it, and a longing for the intact home to be restored. As these concepts demonstrate, it is difficult to overstate the importance of "home" to human life and community. (On the other hand, we can recall German philosopher Theodor Adorno's belief that I referred to earlier, that the highest form of morality is not to be comfortable in one's own home.)

But what constitutes "home" for individuals or communities in our highly mobile society? I've read that once we have truly lived in many places we cannot put ourselves fully together in one place again — a small piece of our emotional heart remains in those other places. At first I took that to mean that we could never again feel that we had a home. But when I was asked to give a convocation speech at Macquarie University in Sydney, Australia, I came to a different conclusion. I called the speech, about my experience of being an expatriate Australian, "Leaving Homes." I had realized, with some surprise, that whichever direction I flew across the Pacific Ocean, whether from Montreal to Sydney or Sydney to Montreal, when friends on either continent asked me where I was going, I said, "I'm going home." And I was, in both cases. I realized it's possible to have more than one "true" home.

Geography professors J. Douglas Porteous and Sandra Smith have written a book called *Domicide: The Global Destruction of Home*. In the abstract for their book, they write: "Media reports describing the destruction of people's homes, for reasons ranging from ethnic persecution to the perceived need for a new airport or highway, are all too familiar. The planned destruction of homes affects millions of people globally; places destroyed range in scale from single dwellings to entire homelands. Domicide tells how and why the powerful destroy homes that happen to be in the way of corporate, political, bureaucratic, and strategic projects. Too frequently, this destruction is justified as being in the public interest."[38] A *Globe and Mail* review of the book summed up the authors' point this way: "Their [the developers'] eyes see rubble, former exiles see home."[39]

I wonder how the concept of home — and loss of home — might relate to finding a shared ethics. Are we currently "homeless" ethically because we have difficulty finding shared values in a pluralistic, secular society, let alone in the world at large? It is true that humans have never had one shared ethic to guide them; rather, we have always been divided between a plurality of religions and cultures (granted, with some overlapping customs or "truths"). But humankind's differences were less obvious before modern media and communications technologies brought the world into our homes on a daily basis. Consequently, our present reality in this regard might be different in kind, not just degree, from the past.

I wonder also if we might need to feel we have a physical, emotional, and spiritual home before we can experience belonging to, or believing in, something larger than ourselves. That is, we need to be grounded physically, mentally, emotionally, and spiritually before we can enter a larger entity and satisfy our need for transcendence. To address more specifically the question of how we might bring past virtues to a future world, we need to ask two other questions: Might experiencing transcendence be a necessary condition before we can act virtuously? And, paradoxically, do we need to experience transcendence to fully experience our own unique selves?

• • •

I started this book as a journey with the intent of mapping out paths we could follow to find a shared ethics — ethics that would respect life and the human spirit. In this last chapter, I have suggested some old virtues that might assist us as we walk those paths. Which brings me to identify the feature that is common to all of the concepts explored in this chapter: the concept of balance, and the idea that achieving balance is an ongoing process, not an event.

We began by looking at complexity — which can make balance seem difficult to achieve or maintain. Sometimes complexity is not present or needed, and the simple (as opposed to the simplistic) is the ethical way forward. Other times, we must try to deal — in equanimity — with the uncertainty complexity entails. Then we need to balance virtues with certain restraints: trust with healthy doubt; courage with good judgement and caution; compassion with "tough love"; generosity with prudence; and hope with realism. And sometimes we have to prioritize values as expressed in virtues — for example, occasionally courage may need to take priority over trust. Making decisions as to when that is ethical and when it is not is at the heart of "doing ethics."

One definition of a sense of humour is that it is a mechanism to achieve dynamic balance: we don't take ourselves too seriously, but neither are we frivolous; we can see the other side even when we believe firmly in our own position; we are "on the one hand/on the other hand" people.

I once gave a speech I called "Gazing at Stars and Patting Cats." Its theme was that in order to live with equanimity and hope, to experience awe, wonder and joy, and to deal with our tragedies, despairs, and sorrows, we humans need to have one hand patting an animal or in the earth, and the other hand reaching out to the stars — to the universe. In doing both, we are in contact with nature — with its intimacy and closeness on the one hand, and its grandeur and vastness on the other. It is no accident that we often speak of the need to be "grounded," and that is no less a requirement in our search for a shared ethics than in undertaking any other fundamentally important human activity. Moreover, the farther out we mean to travel, whether intellectually, imaginatively, emotionally, or spiritually, the deeper our grounding should be if we are to travel safely.

We are the new generation of explorers of our human mind, imagination, and spirit. The challenge for all of us is to create structures with which we can personally identify and in which we can feel we belong, and yet which allow us to recognize ourselves and all others as part of one human family. This book looks at some of the matters we might think about and some of the means we might use in trying to create that structure. I believe that our best chance of finding a shared ethics is, first, to open up what we might call a "dialectic possibility" — that is, the possibility of debate involving both our imaginations and our intellects; second, to invoke all our ways of knowing, but especially the imagination as a guide to ethical thinking; and third, to appeal to our poetic, moral, and spiritual senses directly — in other words, without too much dialectic. I'm trying to build bridges among these often isolated ways of knowing and ways of going about knowing. Guided by our ethical imagination, we must continue to journey on the ethical wallaby in search of our human spirit and the richness of meaning it brings us.

"I have learned two lessons in my life: first, there are no sufficient literary, psychological, or historical answers to human tragedy, only moral ones. Second, just as despair can come to one another only from other human beings, hope, too, can be given to one only by other human beings."

— Elie Wiesel

ACKNOWLEDGEMENTS

I AM DEEPLY grateful to the many people who have contributed in various ways to this book and to the production of the Massey Lectures.

First, I want to thank my research assistant Patrick Murdoch. In particular, the structured conversations we engaged in throughout the summer of 2005 were invaluable in developing this text. I learnt much. I also thank my colleague, friend, and oft-times editor Paul Nathanson — the Wordwatcher — for his stringent criticism, suggestions and generous assistance.

Among the "Massey Lectures Mob" from the CBC *Ideas* team, Philip Coulter deserves very special thanks for his skill in identifying the "big picture" I was trying to bring out of the shadows and helping me to articulate it, as well as for his unusual blend of kindness and severity as a consultant and editor. Many thanks also to Bernie Lucht, who persuaded me to embark on this project and offered often-much-needed support. I am deeply grateful to my editor Lynn Henry, from House of Anansi Press, for her insightful questions and editing which have enriched the book. And my thanks go to John Fraser Master of Massey College for encouragement in stressful times.

My friends have been, as always, patient and supportive in listening to endless "trial runs" of ideas on my part. I thank them all, but special thanks go to Montrealers Katherine Young, Norbert Gilmore, Donald Boudreau, Germaine Gibara, Irene Simons, Marie Giguère, Tom Warn, Marc Berthiaume, Richard Cruess, and Sylvia Cruess; and Aussies Anne McDonell, Mary Brooksbank, Frank Brennan and Geraldine Hawkes. Among colleagues at the Faculty of Law at McGill University, as dean, Nicholas Kasirer has been unfailingly supportive, and Desmond Manderson and Roderick Macdonald have cheerfully acted as "corridor meetings" sounding boards.

Julie Fontaine provided excellent secretarial and administrative assistance — and hard-to-find references - and I thank her and Eileen Parle, who, as ever, was always available in the wings.

My thanks go to the John Dobson Foundation Fund for a grant that supported Patrick Murdoch's research assistance.

Finally, with gratitude for my in-house connection to nature — Ozone and Didjeridon't.

NOTES

Chapter 1

1. Blair, Tony. "Our values are our guide." *Globe and Mail*, May 27, 2006, AI5.
2. Somerville, Margaret. *The Ethical Canary: Science, Society, and the Human Spirit.* Toronto: Penguin, 2000.
3. For a comprehensive discussion of a contemporary natural law theory that can accommodate both those with a belief in God and those without, see: Finnis, John. *Natural Law and Natural Rights.* Oxford: Oxford University Press, 1980.
4. Garrofo, Volnei. "Applied ethics in the context of the southern hemisphere." *UNESCO, Proceedings, Third Session of the World Commission on the Ethics of Scientific Knowledge and Technology* (COMEST). Rio de Janeiro, Brazil, December 1-4, 2003, 89–93, 91.
5. http://rolheiser.com/arco72405.html.
6. Rolheiser, Ronald. Email message to author, August 14, 2006.

7. Young, Katherine and Paul Nathanson. Forthcoming publication.

8. Carter, Philip. Quoted in *St. Paul's Newsletter*, April 21, 2005. Julian Centre: www.users.senet.com.au/~julianc.

9. Forster, E. M. "Aspects of the Novel." As cited by Richard Rorty, *Philosophy and Social Hope*. London: Penguin Group, 1999, 224.

10. Somerville, Margaret. "A post-modern moral tale: The ethics of research relationships." *Nature Reviews Drug Discovery* 2002; 1: 316–320.

11. Scruton, Roger. "A Carnivore's Credo," from R. Scruton, "Eating Your Friends." *Harper's*, April/May 2006: 21–26.

12. *Ibid*.

13. Ralston Saul, John. *The Unconscious Civilization*. Toronto: House of Anansi Press, 1995.

14. Ralston Saul, John. *On Equilibrium*. New York: Penguin/Viking, 2001.

15. Somerville, Margaret A. "Labels versus Contents: Variance between Philosophy, Psychiatry and Law in Concepts Governing Decision-Making." (1994) 39 *McGill Law Journal:* 179–199.

16. Tillich, Paul. *Systematic Theology, Volumes 1–3*. Chicago: University of Chicago Press, 1951, 1957, and 1963. Vol. 1, 71–75.

17. Somerville, Margaret A. "Justice across the generations." *Social Science & Medicine* 29(3) (1989): 385–394.

18. Colloquium on AIDS, Health, and Human Rights. "The Right to Health: A Human Rights Perspective." *Modern Health and Human Rights*. Fondation Marcel Merieux, Institut des Sciences du Vivant, Veyrier-du-Lac (Annecy), France. See also Margaret A. Somerville, "Human Rights and Human Ethics: Health and Health Care" in *Death Talk:*

The Case Against Euthanasia and Physician-assisted Suicide. Montreal: McGill-Queens University Press, 2002, 327-343.

19. Little, Miles. "Ethics, Law, and Technology — More than the Doctor's Dilemma." *The Ethics of Innovation, The Alfred Deakin Innovation Lectures*, April 29 – May 12, 2005. Melbourne: Melbourne University Press, forthcoming, May 2007.

20. See Rorty, Richard. *Supra* note 7, 263–277. Rorty proposes we should give up the fruitless search for "the" Truth.

21. Jacobs, Jane. *Systems of Survival*. New York: Vintage, 1994.

22. See Rawls, John. *Political Liberalism*. New York: Columbia University Press, 1993. Rawls discusses his concept of overlapping consensuses.

23. Wright, Robert. *The Moral Animal: Why We Are the Way We Are: The New Science of Evolutionary Psychology*. Toronto: Random House, 1995.

24. Weaver, Ian C. G., Nadia Cervoni, Frances A. Champagne, Ana C. D'Alessio, Shakti Sharma, Jonathan R. Seckl, Sergiy Dymov, Moshe Szyf, Michael J. Meaney. "Epigenetic programming by maternal behavior," *Nature Neuroscience* 2004; 7 (8): 847–854.

25. *Quirks and Quarks*. CBC Radio, July 30, 2005.

26. Franklin, John. Quoted in Sten Nadolny, *The Discovery of Slowness*. Translated by Ralph Freedman. Edinburgh: Canongate, 2003, 260.

27. Habermas, Jürgen. *The Future of Human Nature*. Cambridge: Polity Press, 2003, 11, 37–44.

Chapter 2

1. Somerville, Margaret. *The Ethical Canary: Science, Society, and the Human Spirit*. Toronto: Penguin, 2000.

2. Lewis, Stephen. *Race Against Time*. Toronto: House of Anansi Press, 2005.

3. Somerville, Margaret A. and Ronald M. Atlas. "Ethics: A Weapon to Counter Bioterrorism." *Science* 2005; 307: 1881–1882.

4. Brooks, Rodney A. *Flesh and Machines*. New York: Pantheon, 2002.

5. Note that both Singer and Brooks are utilitarians.

6. Yankelovich, Daniel. "Trends in American Cultural Values." *Criterion* (August 1996): 2–9.

7. Shields, Carol. *Larry's Party*. New York: Viking/Penguin, 2000, 179.

8. "The Mystical Imagination." http://ronrolheiser.com/arc072405.html, July 24, 2005. Commenting on Wendy Wright's *Sacred Heart, Gateway to God*. Maryknoll, NY: Orbis Books, 2001.

9. Watson, Don. *Death Sentences*. New York: Gotham Books, 2005.

10. Somerville, Margaret A. "Labels vs Contents: Variance between Philosophy, Psychiatry and Law in Concepts Governing Decision-Making." *McGill Law Journal* 39 (1994): 179–199.

11. Doucet, Clive. "A letter to my daughter on the nation of my heart." *Globe and Mail*, June 30, 2005, A19.

12. I'm indebted to my research assistant, Patrick Murdoch, for suggesting the latter image.

13. Parfitt, Derek. *Reasons and Persons*. Oxford: Oxford University Press, 1984.

14. Nafisi, Azar. *Reading Lolita in Tehran*. New York: Random House, 2004, 94.

15. Lonergan, Bernard. *Insight: A Study of Human Understanding*. New York: Philosophical Library, 1970.

16. Habermas, Jürgen. *The Future of Human Nature.* Cambridge: Polity Press, 2003, 10–11.

17. *Ibid.*

18. King James Bible, 1:1 John.

19. Gilmore, Norbert, and Margaret A. Somerville. "Stigmatization, Scapegoating and Discrimination in Sexually Transmitted Diseases: Overcoming 'Them' and 'Us'." *Social Science & Medicine* (9) 1994; 39: 1339–1358.

20. I have always longed to be a poet, so it pleases me to think an ethicist might have something in common with a poet.

21. I'm indebted to Patrick Murdoch for this insight.

Chapter 3

1. See, for example, Rorty, Richard. *Philosophy and Social Hope.* London: Penguin Group, 1999.

2. Schmidt, Larry with Scott Marratto. *The End of Ethics in a Technological Society.* Montreal: McGill-Queen's University Press, forthcoming, 2007, Chapter 6.

3. Dawkins, Richard. *The Selfish Gene.* Oxford: Oxford University Press, 1989.

4. Wilson, Edward O. *Consilience: The Unity of Knowledge.* New York, Toronto: Alfred A. Knopf Inc., 1998; Dawkins, *ibid.*

5. Haraway, Donna. *Primate Visions: Gender, Race, and Nature in the World of Modern Science.* New York, London: Routledge, 1989; Kitzinger, Celia. *Changing Our Minds.* London: Onlywomen Press, 1993; Berger, Peter L. and Thomas Luckmann. *The Social Construction of Reality.* New York: Doubleday, 1966; Pinker, Steven. *The Blank Slate: The Modern Denial of Human Nature.* New York: Viking Penguin, 2002.

6.   For a contrary view, see: Flintoft, Louisa. "Neurogenetics: A male gene for a male brain." *Nature Reviews Genetics 7* (April 2006) 244–245.

7.   Somerville, Margaret. "What About the Children?" in Daniel Cere and Douglas Farrow (eds.) *Divorcing Marriage*. Montreal: McGill-Queens University Press, 2004, 99–115.

8.   President's Council on Bioethics, Human Cloning and Human Dignity. *An ethical inquiry*. Washington, D.C.: President's Council on Bioethics, Human Cloning and Human Dignity, July 2002. www.bioethics.gov/topics/cloning_index.html (accessed December 8, 2003).

9.   Scruton, Roger. "A Carnivore's Credo," from R. Scruton, "Eating Your Friends." *Harper's* (April/May 2006) 21–26.

10. Scully, Matthew. *Dominion: The Power of Man, the Suffering of Animals, and the Call to Mercy*. New York: St. Martin's Press, 2002.

11. Sloane, Karel. "A View of Nature." *Arts & Opinion 5* (2) (2006).

12. *Ibid*.

13. Banks, Deborah. "Mother nature needs more city boys and girls." *Globe and Mail,* November 4, 2003, A22.

14. LeDoux, Joseph. *The Emotional Brain*. New York: Simon and Schuster, 1996.

15. Press, Joy. "Wander Woman." *Village Voice*, June 28, 2005.

16. *Ibid*.

17. Durkheim, Emile. *Suicide: A Study in Sociobiology*. Translated by J.A. Spalding and G. Simpson. Glencoe, IL: Free Press, 1951.

18. Ricoeur, Paul. *Oneself as Another*. Translated by K. Blamey. Chicago: University of Chicago Press, 1992.

19. Macklin, Ruth. "Dignity is a useless concept." *BMJ 327* (2003): 1419–1420.

20. *Ibid*. Citing (U.S.) President's Council on Bioethics, Human Cloning and Human Dignity. *An ethical inquiry.* Washington, D.C.: President's Council on Bioethics, Human Cloning and Human Dignity, July 2002.

21. Schweitzer, Albert. *Civilization and Ethics.* C.T. Campion. London: A & C Black, 1949.

22. Albrecht, Glenn. "Organicism and the Organic University." *Concresence: The Australian Journal for Process Thought*, 6 (2005) [C1]: 1–16.

23. Albrechit, *ibid.,* citing Worster, Donald. *Nature's Economy: The Roots of Ecology.* San Francisco: Sierra Club Books, 1977, 333.

24. Albrecht, Glenn. "From Jungle Fowl to Factory Flesh: Changing Perspectives on the Chicken in Contemporary Society." Eds. D. Balnave et al., *Proceedings of the Australia Poultry Science Symposium.* Sydney: University of Sydney 13: 43–50.

25. Highfield, H. and N. Flemming. "An egg has been tricked into dividing: Scientists create human embryo without a father." *National Post*, September 10, 2005, A2.

26. *The Assisted Human Reproduction Act*, S.C. 2004, c.2.

27. Abboud, Amin. "Inside the Secret World of IVF." *The* [Melbourne] *Age,* May 6, 2005. http://www.theage.com.au/news/Opinion/Inside-the-secret-world-of-IVF/2005/05 (accessed May 18, 2005).

28. El Akkad, Omar. "Miracle baby gives men pregnant pause." *Globe and Mail*, September 27, 2005, A15.

29. Hamer, Dean. "NIH Links Sexuality to Genetic Factor." http://www.cs.cmu.edu/ats/cs/user/scotts/bulgarian/nih-upi.html (November 8, 1998).

30. Menzies, Heather. "Age cannot wither us — can it?" Review of *The Long Tomorrow: How Advances in Evolutionary Biology Can Help Us Postpone Aging*, by Michael R. Rose. *Globe and Mail*, November 19, 2005, D4.

31. Somerville, Margaret. *Death Talk: The Case Against Euthanasia and Physician-Assisted Suicide*. Montreal: McGill-Queen's University Press, 2002.

32. Singer, Peter and Abdallah Daar. "We should clone this UK policy." *Globe and Mail*, August 12, 2004, A17.

33. Sheth, S.S. "Missing Female Births in India." *The Lancet* 2006; 367: 185–186.

34. Habermas, Jürgen. *The Future of Human Nature*. Oxford: Blackwell Publishing, 2003, vii, 32.

35. Mundy, Lisa. "Souls on Ice." http://www.motherjones.com/news/feature/2006/07/soulsonice.html.

36. Velleman, J. David. "Family History." *Philosophical Papers* 34 (2005): 357–378.

37. See, for instance, Skelton, Chad. "Searching for their genes: Family Ties." *Vancouver Sun*, April 22, 2006.

38. Ishiguro, Kazuo. *Never Let Me Go*. Toronto: Vintage Canada, 2006.

39. *Marriage for Civil Purposes Act*, S.C. 2005, c.33

40. *Ibid.*, "Consequential Amendments," sections 5–15; Makin, Kirk. "Two mothers should be allowed on birth document, judge says." *Globe and Mail*, June 7, 2006, A10.

41. Kerjab, Richard. "Wife gets sperm of dead husband." *The Australian*, December 21, 2005, 3.

Chapter 4

1. May, William F. *The Patient's Ordeal*. Bloomington: Indiana University Press, 1991, 9–10.

2. Warnke, Patrick H. "Repair of a human face by allotransplantation." *Lancet* 2006; 368: 181–82. See also: Edgardo D. Carosella, T. Pradeu. "Transplantation and Identity: a dangerous split." *Lancet* 2006; 368: 183–84.

3. Wade, Nicholas. "Scientists say they've found a code beyond genetics in DNA." *New York Times*, July 25, 2006.

4. Brooks, Rodney A. *Flesh and Machines: How Robots Will Change Us*. New York: Pantheon, 2002.

5. Singer, Peter. *Animal Liberation*. Toronto: HarperCollins Canada/Harper Trade, reprint edition, 2001.

6. Visser, Margaret. *Beyond Fate*. Toronto: House of Anansi Press, 2002, 84.

7. Brooks, Rodney A. *Supra*, note 4.

8. Clisham, Michael. "Refining Humanity: A Review of *The Coevolution of Human Potential and Converging Technologies*." *The Journal of Law Medicine & Ethics* 33 (2005): 380–383. See also, M. C. Roco and C. D. Montemagno, eds. *The Coevolution of Human Potential and Converging Technologies*. New York: The New York Academy of Sciences, 2004.

9. Clisham. *Ibid.*, 381.

10. Associated Press. "Scientists pack power into tongues." *The* [Montreal] *Gazette*, April 25, 2006, A16.

11. Somerville, Margaret A. and Ronald M. Atlas. "Ethics: A Weapon to Counter Bioterrorism." *Science* 2005; 307: 1881–1882.

12. http://www.americanhumanist.org/index.html (accessed August 22, 2005).

13. The passages in quotation marks in this section are from the transhumanist website www.betterhumans.com, or links to it.

14. Somerville, Margaret. *Death Talk: The Case against Euthanasia and Physician-Assisted Suicide*. Montreal: McGill-Queen's University Press, 2002, 113.

15. See www.betterhumans.com.

16. Brooks, Rodney A. *supra*, note 7.

17. Lewis, Joanne. "Older brain often faster: report." *The* [Montreal] *Gazette*, February 5, 2005, A16.

18. August 2–4, 2006, Rio de Janeiro. Organized by the Institute for Social Medicine (State University of Rio de Janeiro) and the Max Planck Institute for the History of Science (Berlin).

19. See the Chinese proverb in Chapter 1.

20. Rothenberg, David. "Music on your mind." *Globe and Mail*, July 29, 2006, D8–D9.

21. Domurat Dreger, Alice. *One of Us: Conjoined Twins and the Future of Normal*. Cambridge MA: Harvard University Press, 2005.

22. The American philosopher Richard Rorty, for instance, decries a search for truth as leading us astray ethically. Rorty, Richard. *Philosophy and Social Hope*. London: Penguin Group, 1999, 262–277.

Chapter 5

1. Plsek, Paul E. and Tim Wilson. "Complexity science: complexity, leadership, and management in healthcare organizations." *BMJ 323* (2001): 746–749. Full text online: http://bmj.bmjjournals.com/cgi/content/full/323/7315/746.

2. Berlin, Isaiah. *Liberty*. Henry Hardy, ed. Oxford, New York: Oxford University Press, 2002, 213.

3. Notes from an interview by Michael Enright with Charles Taylor, CBC Radio *This Morning*, December 5, 1999.

4. Katz, Jay. *The Silent World of Doctor and Patient*. New York: The Free Press, 1984.

5. Riley, Susan. "Elected officials talk to us like they think we are stupid." *The* [Montreal] *Gazette*, June 1, 2006, A17.

6. Somerville, Margaret A. "Social-Ethical Values Issues in the Political Public Square: Principles vs. Packages." *The Journal of Law, Medicine & Ethics* 32 (2004): 731–740.

7. Jacobs, Jane. *Systems of Survival: A Dialogue on the Moral Foundations of Commerce and Politics*. Toronto: Vintage, 1992.

8. Habermas, Jürgen. *The Future of Human Nature*. Cambridge: Polity Press, 2003.

9. *Ibid.*, vii.

10. *Ibid.*, viii, 91.

11. *Ibid.*, 97.

12. *Arndt v. Smith*, [1997] 2 S.C.R. 539 (Supreme Court of Canada).

13. Somerville, Margaret A. "Justice Across the Generations." *Social Science & Medicine,* 1989; 29(3):385-394.

14. Ishiguro, Kazuo. *Never Let Me Go*. Toronto: Vintage Canada, 2006.

15. http://www.cbc.ca/correspondent/feature_050313.html.

16. Malinas, Gary and John Bigelow. In *The Stanford Encyclopedia of Philosophy*, E. N. Zalta, ed., Stanford, CA: The Metaphysics Research Lab, 2004; available at http://plato.stanford.edu/archives/spr2004/entries/paradox-simpson/

17. Armstrong, Karen. "The Great Transformation." Beatty Memorial Lecture, McGill University, Montreal, April 27, 2006.

18. Somerville, Margaret. "Feat first isn't the ideal attitude for climbers." *The Australian*, June 1, 2006.

19. Carey, Benedict. "When Death is on the Docket, the Moral Compass Wavers." *New York Times*, February 7, 2006. http://www.nytimes.com/2006/02/07/health/psychology/07exec.html?ei=5070&en=f99395c0d6154603&ex=1139979600&emc=eta1&pagewanted=print.

20. Somerville, Margaret A. "Social-Ethical Values Issues in the Political Public Square: Principles vs. Packages." *The Journal of Law, Medicine & Ethics* 32 (2004): 731–740.

21. Sherwin, Susan. *No Longer Patient: Feminist Ethics & Health Care*. Philadelphia: Temple University Press, 1992, 46–52, 80–81.

22. Langford, Dale et al. "Social Modulation of Pain as Evidence for Empathy in Mice." *Science* 2006; 312: 1967–1970.

23. Ritter, Malcolm. "I feel your pain . . . and I like it." *Globe and Mail*, January 18, 2006 (Insider Edition).

24. DiTommaso, Lorenzo. "Identifying 'Us' and 'Them'." *The* [Montreal] *Gazette*, June 23, 2006, J5.

25. Somerville, Margaret A. and Sarah Wilson. "Crossing Boundaries: Travel, Immigration, Human Rights, and AIDS." (1998) 43 *McGill Law Journal*: 781–834.

26. *Beliefnet*, May 2000. www.beliefnet.com.

27. *Ibid*, citing Paul Wilkes. *Beyond the Walls: Monastic Wisdom for Everyday Life*. New York: Image, 2000.

28. Kant, Immanuel. *Perpetual Peace: A Philosophical Essay*. Translated by M. Campbell Smith. New York; Garland, 1972.

29. Dickinson, Emily. *The Complete Poems of Emily Dickinson*. Boston: Little, Brown, 1924; Bartelby.com, 2000. www.bartelby.com/113/. Accessed August 2, 2006.

30. Ganzini, L., W. S. Johnston, B. H. McFarland, S. W. Tolle, M. A. Lee. "Attitudes of patients with amyotrophic lateral

sclerosis and their care givers toward assisted suicide." *New England Journal of Medicine*, 1998; 339: 967–973. See also Chochinov, H. M., L. Ganzini, W. S. Johnston. "Patients with amyotrophic lateral sclerosis and physician-assisted suicide." *New England Journal of Medicine*, 1999; 340: 817. Correspondence.

31. Somerville, Margaret. "Death of Pain: Pain, Suffering, and Ethics." *Progress in Pain Research and Management*. Eds. Gerald E Gebhart, Donna L. Hammond, and Troels S. Jensen, vol. 2, 41–58. *Proceedings of the 7th World Congress on Pain*. Seattle, WA.: International Association for the Study of Pain Press, 1994. Also published in Margaret Somerville, *Death Talk: The Case Against Euthanasia and Physician-Assisted Suicide*. Montreal: McGill-Queen's University Press, 2002.

32. Kennedy, Robert F. "A Tiny Ripple of Hope." Day of Affirmation Address at Cape Town University. Delivered June 6, 1966, Cape Town, South Africa. http://www.americanrhetoric.com/speeches/rfk-capetown.htm.

33. Troy, Gil. "Good neighbours, good friends." *The* [Montreal] *Gazette*, July 4, 2005, A19.

34. Somerville, Margaret. *The Ethical Canary: Science, Society and the Human Spirit*. Toronto: Penguin, 2000, xvi.

35. Sahtouris, Elisabet. "Humanity 3000 Participant Statement." Foundation for the Future. http://www.ratical.org/LifeWeb/Articles/humanity3000.html

36. Swimme, Brian. *Canticle to the Cosmos*. Audiocassette, Sounds True Productions, March 1996.

37. Nathanson, Paul. *Over the Rainbow: The Wizard of Oz As a Secular Myth of America*. Albany: State University of New York Press, 1992.

38. Porteous, J. Douglas and Sandra J. Smith. *Domicide: The Global Destruction of Home*. Montreal: McGill-Queen's University Press, 2001.

39. Koring, Paul. "The eyes see rubble, former exiles see home: Lebanese forced to flee 22 years ago celebrate coming back to the village of their fathers." *The Globe and Mail*, 23 June 2000, A12.

INDEX